NetApp ONTAP

administration

Command-line
by example

For Aleks and Monique.

About the author.

Peter van der Weerd is a UNIX/Linux/NetApp trainer and consultant. He has been a contractor since 1995 and worked for companies like Sun Microsystems, Hewlett Packard, IBM and other IT companies in the Netherlands and abroad.

Printed in 2019

The argument for this document.

This book takes a shot at urging administrators to the command-line interface of the ONTAP operating system. NetApp offers multiple graphical user interfaces to administer their products. Graphical user interfaces can very often be welcome for common administration and user-friendly overviews. But not all work can be done with graphical user interfaces. Sometimes you will have to use the command-line. Next to that it can be argued that working with the command-line gives the administrator a better understanding of how ONTAP – or any other operating system for that matter – works.

This book does not aim to cover all aspects of the ONTAP operating system in depth, but it does try to cover day-to-day administration of the ONTAP cluster by means of command-line examples. Every module – except the first one – starts with a short introduction of the topic(s) at hand and then some examples are worked out. These examples are all executed on a virtualized environment. The environment consists of two NetApp clusters, a windows client and a linux client. In a virtualized environment, most of what you do in real life can be simulated. The primary disadvantages of working with NetApp simulators are twofold:

1. You cannot run FibreChannel connections.

2. It is a shared-nothing environment, so Storage Failover is not supported. Every node in a cluster has its own disks.

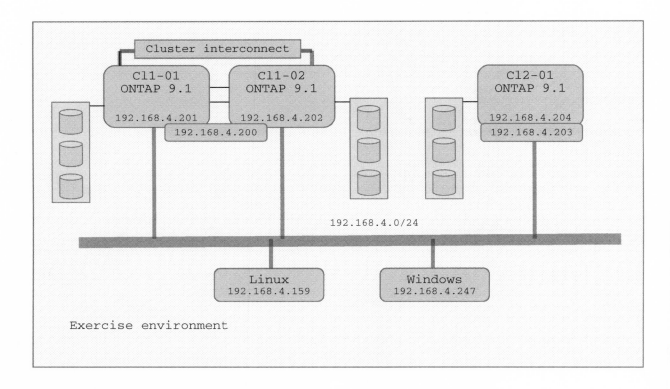

Typography.

Text is printed in 'Times New Roman' size 11. Sometimes, to stress or attract attention, words will be printed in *italic*. Commands and pathnames in text are printed in **`courier size 10 bold`**.

Lists are presented in tables, the text in lists if courier size 10.

header	header
Example2	List

Examples are presented in Frames, font `courier size 10`.

```
systemprompt::> command
command output is not bold
```

Footers are printed in Times New Roman size 8.

Notes are printed in font **Times New Roman size 9 bold**.

Most modules end with a **'TRY THIS'** section. These sections contain questions and assignments. The answer key to these sections can be found in Appendix A.

Disclaimer.

Init can not be held responsible for problems caused by copying parts of this book to an actual production environment.

The online training-version of this book can be obtained at:

https://www.udemy.com/netapp-ontap-command-line-administration/

Table of Contents

Table of Contents

1. Concepts and Architecture.

This module discusses the NetApp architecture. It will focus on what a NetApp Cluster is, how communication between the clusternodes is organized, where the configuration is stored and how data flows within the cluster. Basic concepts like aggregates, volumes and other objects will also be touched upon. The different concepts will be dealt with in more depth in other modules.

1.1 Cluster.

A cluster can be as small as a single node or as large as twenty-four nodes. A node is a controller that runs the ONTAP operating system. The fact that a single controller is also called a cluster, may seem strange. However, nodes can be added to or removed from the cluster on the fly at any time. So a single node cluster is not something which has to be a permanent situation. Adding nodes to an existing cluster is called *scaling out*. If you were to add more disk shelves to an existing single node cluster or to a pair of nodes, you would be *scaling up*.

1.2 HA-Pair.

A single node cluster that is scaled out, is paired with a second node via a so-called HA-Interconnect and a Cluster Interconnect (1.3). The HA-Interconnect is a network between two nodes that is used to mirror the contents of the controller's Non-volatile RAM (NVRAM) or Non-volatile Memory (NVMEM) to the other node in the HA-Pair and vice versa. Also, the two nodes will have physical access to the same disk shelves. A multi-node cluster is a collection of one or more HA-Pairs. The maximum number of HA-pairs primarily depends on the protocols used. In a NAS environment the maximum number is twelve HA-Pairs. In a SAN environment the maximum is limited to six HA-Pairs[1].

1.3 Cluster Interconnect.

A single HA-Pair is *interconnected* – next to the HA-Interconnect – by a network that is called Cluster Interconnect. This network has a minimum of two 10Gb network interfaces per physical node. The nodes in a single HA-Pair can be interconnected point to point or by means of two dedicated switches. Multiple HA-Pairs forming one cluster, will always be interconnected by using dedicated switches. The Cluster Interconnect network is used for all communication between the nodes of one cluster. This entails configuration information, cluster heartbeat, block replication and volume data.

The following picture shows a single node cluster, a single HA-Pair cluster, and a 4-node cluster. All three forms can be scaled out on the fly, by adding a second node to the single node cluster or by adding more HA-Pairs to a multi-node cluster. If a cluster is not a single node cluster, the number of nodes is always even. The cluster interconnect network can be point-to-point or switched. Obviously, it can only be point-to-point in a cluster with a single HA-Pair.

Note: nodes can also be removed from a cluster by *unjoining*. Both nodes of the HA-Pair will have to be unjoined and can only be re-used after initializing all disks.

---

1   These numbers, as the majority of numbers in this document, are subject to change as ONTAP evolves.

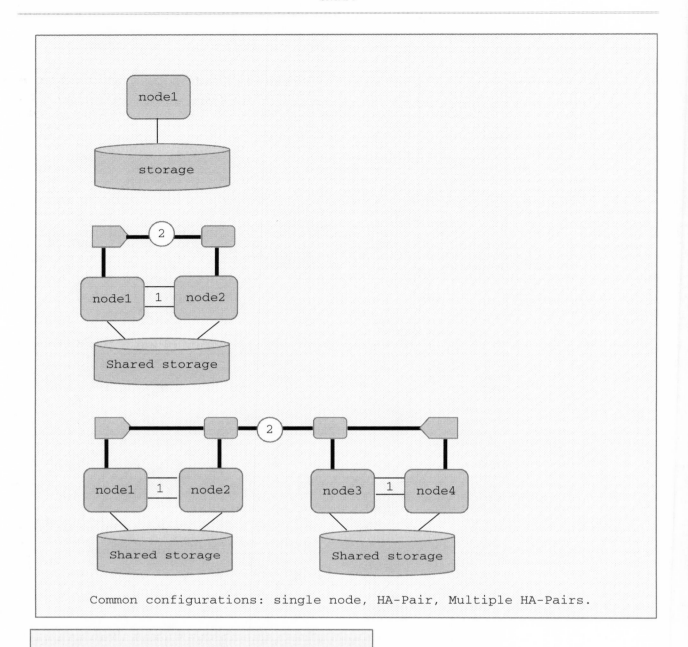

Common configurations: single node, HA-Pair, Multiple HA-Pairs.

1=HA-Interconnect (nvram mirroring)
Usually connected via backplane.

2=Cluster Interconnect (cluster traffic)
10Gb dedicated network
2 ports per node.

Management network and
Data network are not shown.

1.4 Aggregates.

An aggregate is a collection of physical hard disk drives or solid state drives, or a combination of the two. A node always has a minimum of one aggregate which is called the *root aggregate*. This root aggregate has one volume (see 1.5) for configuration data and log files. Obviously every node usually has one or more additional aggregates for storing client data. Aggregates can be grown in size by adding more disks, but they can never be shrunk. An aggregate is managed by one controller only but can be taken over by the other controller in the HA-Pair at node failure or shutdown. This failing over of aggregates is called *Storage Failover*. An HA-Pair is sometimes referred to as a *Storage Fail Over Pair*.

Redundancy of data in an aggregate is realized by creating one or multiple stripes of disks that have a parity-type to safeguard against the loss of one or more drives in a stripe. NetApp refers to a stripe of disks as

a *RaidGroup*. The parity-type of raid groups can be any of the form Raid-4, Raid-DP or Raid-Tec, respectively single parity, double parity and triple parity. ONTAP does not protect agains the loss of a disk shelf unless you run a *Metro Cluster*. Metro Clusters are not discussed in this book.

1.5 Volumes.

A volume is the placeholder for data inside an aggregate. Data of any form is always stored in a volume. In other words: no data without the use of volumes.

1.5.1 Root Volume.

Every node has a root volume which is called *vol0*. This volume contains log files, backup files and configuration information. This volume is mounted at boot time and the node is only functional after the root volume is mounted. A node that loses its root volume is a dysfunctional node and needs to be recovered.

1.5.2 Data Volume.

A data volume contains user data. Data volumes are stored in data aggregates. Data volumes can grow and shrink in size, either manually or automatically. A data aggregate can contain many volumes with a maximum of up to one thousand per node[1]. Volumes can be moved from one aggregate to any other data aggregate in the cluster. Replication and backing up of data is typically done at the volume level.

1.6 File System.

The UNIX file system that is used by ONTAP is called *WAFL*. WAFL stands for Write Anywhere File Layout. When an aggregate is created, a file system is automatically created in the aggregate. When a volume is created, a separate administrative starting point for that volume is created as if it were a separate file system. So, conceptually, twenty volumes in one single aggregate represent twenty different file systems. Physically however, all the blocks in the different volumes belong to the same aggregate file system. As with all UNIX file systems, to access a file system, it has to be mounted to a directory which is usually referred to as a mount point. In ONTAP, such a mount point is called a junction-path. File systems can by mounted and unmounted at will. Unmounted file system are not accessible by NAS clients.

---

1   One thousand is the absolute maximum. Depending on the controller model the maximum may vary.

1.7 Replicated Databases.

All cluster configuration information is stored locally on every node's root volume (vol0). This information is the same on every node in the cluster. In other words: the Replicated Databases are *in sync*, cluster wide. Every configuration change at the cluster level is always replicated to all nodes in the cluster. This means that every node is aware of every bit of cluster configuration information. This entails volumes, ip-addresses, aggregates, users, policies, schedules and so on and so forth.

Rd	Function
Vldb	The volume location database contains volume and aggregate information.
Vifmgr	The virtual interface manager database contains network information.
Bcomd	The block configuration and operations manager database contains SAN information.
Crs	The configuration replication service database contains SVM configuration data.
Mgmt	The management database contains all configuration that is not stored in the first four databases.

1.8 Logical Interfaces.

A logical interface or *LIF* is a logical entity that holds an IP address or World Wide Port Number. A LIF represents a network access point to a node in the cluster. Lifs can be used for data traffic or management traffic. A lif is always configured on a port.

1.9 Network Ports.

A network port can be a virtual- or physical network port. Physical network ports are network interface cards and host bus adapters. Virtual ports are either groupings of physical ports (interface groups) or VLAN ports.

1.10 Broadcast Domains.

A broadcast domain is a collection of physical and/or virtual ports. Broadcast domains can separate networks to enable secure multi-tenancy. Broadcast domains can also limit the failover possibilities of LIFs. For example, you can create a broadcast domain of VLAN ports only to make sure that a LIF that is configured on a VLAN cannot fail over to an non-VLAN port. Broadcast domains always reside in an *ipspace*.

1.11 Ipspaces.

An *ipspace* is a container. This container holds one or more broadcast domains. At creation time, the ipspace is empty. By populating two different ipspaces with their own physical broadcast domain you can service two identical subnets to two different customers. A cluster at all times has two ipspaces with one broadcast domain each:

The *CLUSTER* ipspace with the CLUSTER broadcast domain.
This ipspace hosts the Cluster Interconnect Network that was discussed in paragraph 1.3. This network is a class B subnet, unless configured otherwise.

The *DEFAULT* ipspace with the DEFAULT broadcast domain.
This ipspace hosts all data subnets.

1.12 Storage Virtual Machine.

A storage virtual machine (SVM), is a cluster-wide container for three entities:
- *Logical Interfaces* (1.8)
- *Volumes* (1.5)
- *Protocols* (nfs,cifs,fcp,iscsi,ndmp)

An SVM can be of the type *system*, *node*, *admin* or *data*. After a new cluster has been setup, there are three SVM-types to start with:

Type	function
Admin SVM.	The cluster setup process automatically creates the admin SVM for the cluster. The admin SVM represents the cluster.
Node SVMs.	A node SVM is created when the node joins the cluster, and the node SVM represents the individual node in the cluster.
System SVM.	A system SVM is automatically created for cluster-level communications in an Ipspace. (cluster interconnect)

1.12.1 Data SVMs.

Data SVMs.	To serve data to NAS and SAN clients.

Data SVMs serve data. After cluster setup, the administrator must create data SVMs and add volumes and LIFS to these SVMs to facilitate data access.

The SVM's original name was *vserver*. This is still reflected in the command-line. The command **vserver** is valid, **svm** is not a command.

1.13 Namespace.

A namespace represents the file system structure of a Data SVM. This means that all volumes that are created in a single SVM form the namespace of that SVM. Volumes in the namespace must have unique names. Two different SVMs may have volumes with the same name since they reside in different namespaces. At the root of the namespace there is a small volume of 1GB that is regarded as the root directory of the namespace. This volume is the root volume of the SVM.

Note: do not confuse the root volume of an SVM with the root volume (vol0) of a node.

The root volume of an SVM typically holds the mountpoints (junction-paths) of volumes mounted in the namespace. The root volume of an SVM should not contain user data.

A junction-path (directory) is automatically created when the datavolume is mounted, and removed when the datavolume is unmounted.

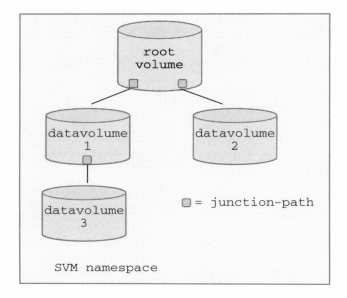

1.14 Flow of a data packet

When a data packet enters the controller via a physical port, the respective module (network/SCSI) will copy it to the Cluster Session Manager (CSM). The CSM will check where the volume resides that needs to receive the data.

If the volume is on the local node, the CSM will copy the data to the DATA-Module. The DATA-Module will write the data to disk.

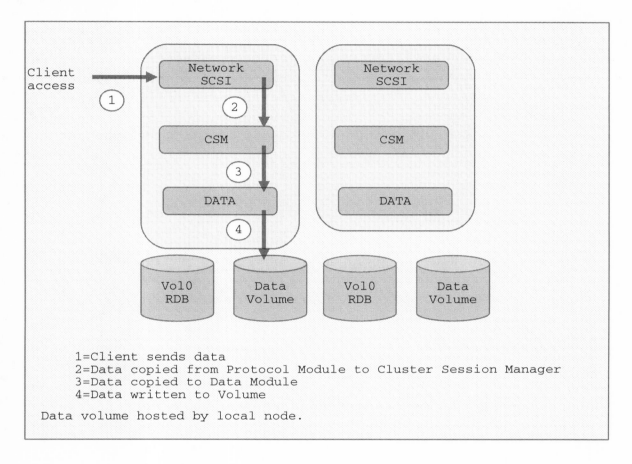

```
1=Client sends data
2=Data copied from Protocol Module to Cluster Session Manager
3=Data copied to Data Module
4=Data written to Volume

Data volume hosted by local node.
```

If the volume is not on the local node, the CSM will copy the data to the node that does hold the volume. The CSM on the remote node copies the data to the DATA-Module. The DATA-Module will write the data to disk .

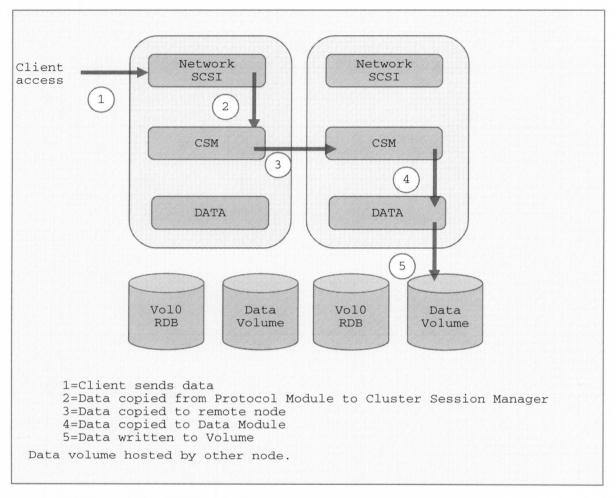

1=Client sends data
2=Data copied from Protocol Module to Cluster Session Manager
3=Data copied to remote node
4=Data copied to Data Module
5=Data written to Volume
Data volume hosted by other node.

Note: the data will be transported to the destination node via the Cluster Interconnect.

As discussed, the location of the volume is stored in the Volume Location Database (VLDB) on vol0.

1.15 NVRAM and NVRAM Mirroring.

After the data packet has reached the node **(1)** that hosts the volume, the data is copied to RAM **(2)**. Then it is copied to NVRAM **(3)**, and to the partner's NVRAM **(4)**. The client is acknowledged that the data is safe **(5)**. For a number of reasons (*NVRAM Full, Snapshot creation, 10 seconds have passed, Memory thresholds, and more*), data will be written to disk by creating a Tetris Block **(6)**, calculating Parity **(7)** and copying it to the storage layer **(8)** that will write the data to disk.

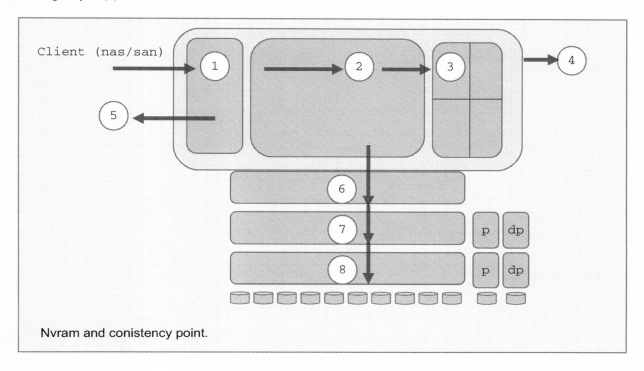

Nvram and conistency point.

After the data has been written to disk, NVRAM is flushed and a Consistency Point is a fact. A consistency point means that a new view of the filesystem is created. Consistency points are discussed in module 7.

If, during the process of writing the blocks, something goes wrong, the complete transaction will be discarded because the root inode was not written. After a reset, NVRAM/NVMEM content is copied into RAM and the transaction is started again, to end with a valid consistency point, and the flushing of NVRAM.

It goes without saying that NVRAM is only NVRAM because it is battery backed-up. If the battery is dangerously low, the system will shutdown in 24 hours. To check the state of the batteries, run the following nodeshell command:

```
cl1::> node run -node cl1-01

cl1_01> environment status chassis
Voltage ok
PSU 1 ok
PSU 2 ok
Temperature ok
System_Fan ok
CF_status ok
NVRAM6-temperature-1 ok
NVRAM6-battery-1 OK
```

If the node that hosts the volume is part of an HA-Pair, the data is not only copied to the local NVRAM, but also mirrored to the partner's NVRAM. Only then will the writing of the data be acknowledged to the client. The rest of the consistency point action, is identical.

1.16 Job Schedules and Policies.

1.16.1 Policies.

ONTAP no longer uses configuration files. All configuration settings are stored in policies an policy rules. A policy can be regarded as a configuration file and a policy rule can be regarded as a line in a configuration file. Every Storage Virtual Machine can have its own policies regarding snapmirror relationships, snapshots, firewalling, quota, et cetera. For most features there are Default policies. You cannot delete Default policies but you can modify them. Policies will be demonstrated in relevant modules.

1.16.2 Job Schedules.

Repetitive task can be scheduled by creating a job schedule and binding it to a policy. Schedules that run on specified times are referred to a *cron schedules* (UNIX). A cron schedule needs a time definition based on minutes of the hour, hours of the day, days of the month, months of the year and day of the week. Schedules that run at intervals are called, *interval schedules*.

The following example creates a schedule that will run a job 10 minutes past 10 o'clock every month of the year, every day of the month and every day of the weak.

```
cl1::> job schedule cron create -name test_sched -minute 10 -hour 10 -month
* -day 1-31 -dayofweek *

cl1::> job schedule show -name test_sched

Schedule Name: test_sched
Schedule Type: cron
  Description: Sun-Sat,Jan-Dec 1-31@10:10
```

2. The Command-line interface.

This module discusses the three available shells and their functions. In addition, user management and Role Based Access Control (RBAC) will be discussed. The reason for that is that accessing the CLI can only be effectuated by allowing particular users to execute particular commands.

2.1 Three shells.

ONTAP has three shells you can work from:

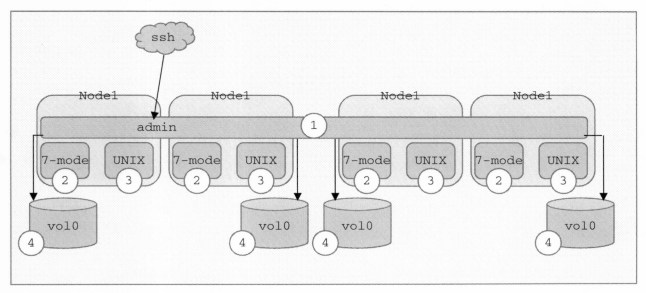

clustershell **(1)** – This is the default shell you login to if you want to configure or manage your cluster. By default ssh is enabled. Every command you execute and every configuration change you make when working in the clustershell, effects all nodes in the cluster[1]. Querying from this shell will gather information that is known throughout the cluster. Applying changes from this shell will update the RDBs on all nodes in the cluster **(4)**. In short: the clustershell manages the entire cluster configuration.

Nodeshell **(2)** – This is the shell that resembles the 7-mode environment. Up to and including ONTAP 8.2, ONTAP was available in two versions: 7-mode (which was functionally identical to ONTAP 7.x), and Clustered ONTAP. As of from 8.3 ONTAP is no longer available in 7-mode. The nodeshell gives access to a limited[2] set of 7-mode commands. Whatever command you use in this shell, it is limited to the node itself.

Systemshell **(3)** – This shell gives you access to UNIX. It is not very likely that you will access this shell unless under guidance of a NetApp Engineer. We are going to discuss this shell though, to make sure that you are familiar with it if you have to go there.

---

1   The relevant replicated database on every node will be updated.
2   With "options nodescope.reenabledcmds" some more commands can be restored. Not recommended.

2.2 The clustershell.

Accessing the clustershell can be done by connecting to the cluster administration IP address or to any of the node IP addresses. You can connect using putty, plink or ssh. In this book we only use a Linux environment as client to manage the cluster from. We login using the *admin* user and run the cluster show command.

The admin user is the default administrator that has full control over the cluster. The password is chosen at installation time and can be changed afterwards.

```
# ssh  admin@192.168.4.200
Password:
cl1::>  cluster show
Node                    Health  Eligibility
--------------------- ------- ------------
cl1-01                  true    true
cl1-02                  true    true
2 entries were displayed.
```

The <tab-key> will give an overview of all commands available. When typing any of the available commands, a subset of commands is opened.

```
cl1::> net <tab-key>
    arp              connections      device-discovery fcp
    interface        ipspace          options          ping
    ping6            port             qos-marking      route
    subnet           traceroute       traceroute6
```

2.2.1 Privilege levels in the clustershell.

The clustershell knows three privilege levels: *admin*, *advanced* and *diagnostic*. The only difference between the levels is that they offer you more or less commands and more or less manual pages, depending on the privilege level. To change from level to level you use the **set** command. See how the prompt changes as you change from privilege level to privilege level. The manual pages give information on how to use a command. The content of the manual pages change as you go down the hierarchical tree of the command sets. For example, the **man vol** command will give you other output than the **man vol create** command.

To go from one privilege level to another:

```
cl1::> set adv

Warning: These advanced commands are potentially dangerous; use
        them only when directed to do so by NetApp personnel.
Do you want to continue? {y|n}: y

cl1::*> set d

Warning: These diagnostic commands are for use by NetApp
        personnel only.
Do you want to continue? {y|n}: y

cl1::*> set admin

cl1::>
```

Typing a command that is not available in the privilege level you are in, will result in a message that the command is *not recognized*. The same goes for accessing the manual page of a command. One thing you could do is, the minute you login, switch to diag mode: **set d**. This way you will never be told that the command is not recognized, unless the command really is not available.

Important keys and arguments in the clustershell:

`<TAB-Key>`	`List possible commands.` `Argument completion.`
`?`	`List possible commands and arguments plus comment.`
`-fields <argument,...>`	`List given properties of an instance.`
`-instance`	`List all properties of an instance.`
`rows 24`	`Show 24 lines output of lines per terminal before pausing. This is formatted output.`
`Rows 0`	`Do not pause the output.` `This is raw output.`

The **top** command will bring you back to the beginning of the hierarchical tree. The **cd ..** command will bring you down one level. You can tab your way to the commands but also type the entire path in one go, if you know the path. So the following command can be achieved by simply tabbing and picking the correct suggestion or by typing it as a whole.

```
Cl1::*>configuration backup create -node cl1-01 -backup-type cluster
-backup-name backup_test
```

2.3 Manual pages.

To find out how to use a command you can use the **man** command. As with the cli itself, the manual pages are also structured hierarchically. This means that, for example, the command **man vol** will give other information than **man vol create**. Also, if the command is not available in a particular privilege level, the manual page for that command is not accessible either.

2.4 History.

The history command will show the instructions that have been executed since the start of the session. Every session has its own history, which will be discarded when logged off.

```
cl1::*> history
    1  set d
    2  history
    3  vserver show
```

2.4.1 Redo.

With the **redo <digit>** command you can rerun an command from the history list.

```
cl1::*> redo 3
                              Admin        Operational Root
Vserver       Type    Subtype State        State       Volume      Aggregate
----------    ------- ------- ----------   ----------- ----------  ----------
Cluster       system  -       -            -           -           -
cl1           admin   -       -            -           -           -
cl1-01        node    -       -            -           -           -
cl1-02        node    -       -            -           -           -
```

2.4 The nodeshell.

The nodeshell gives you access to a limited set of commands that were available in 7-mode. This is a shell that you will not commonly access. Sometimes, experienced users go here to use commands like *sysstat* and *stats*, to retrieve performance information. In previous versions this was the way to manage the root volume of the node, *vol0*. But tunnels have been created so this can be done from the clustershell. So, the need to access the nodeshell is brought down to a minimum.

One way to access the node shell is by typing the **node run -node <nodename>** command.

```
cl1::*> node run -node cl1-02
Type 'exit' or 'Ctrl-D' to return to the CLI
cl1-02> sysstat -i
CPU   NFS    CIFS   iSCSI NET   kB/s  Disk kB/s   iSCSI kB/s Cache
                          in    out   read write in    out   age
60%   0      0      0     8     10    36   694    0     0     >60
61%   0      0      0     3     5     0    0      0     0     >60

cl1-02> exit
```

Another way to run a command in the nodeshell is by passing it on the command line when accessing a node.

```
Cl1::*> node run -node cl1-01 sysstat -i
CPU   NFS    CIFS   iSCSI NET   kB/s  Disk kB/s   iSCSI kB/s Cache
                          in    out   read write in    out   age
60%   0      0      0     8     10    36   694    0     0     >60
61%   0      0      0     3     5     0    0      0     0     >60
```

2.5 The systemshell.

The systemshell is the shell that gives you access to UNIX. Obviously NetApp only wants you to go there under guidance. The systemshell gives access to all files in *vol0*, the compact flash card that holds the kernel and var file system, to all volumes in the entire cluster. In other words, one might say that the systemshell is the entrance to the gold and a shortcut to all of your dreams. Again, NetApp is reluctant to stimulate this.

   Nevertheless, there may come a time that you are on the phone with an engineer and he asks you to access this systemshell for a particular reason. To prepare for that, the diag user has to be unlocked and needs a password.

```
cl1::> security login unlock -username diag
cl1::> security login password -username diag
Enter a new password: ********
Enter it again: ********
```

If needed, you can access the systemshell as follows:

```
cl1::> set d

Warning: These diagnostic commands are for use by NetApp
         personnel only.
Do you want to continue? {y|n}: y

cl1::*> systemshell -node c11-01
   (system node systemshell)
diag@127.0.0.1's password:

Warning:  The systemshell provides access to low-level
diagnostic tools that can cause irreparable damage to
the system if not used properly.  Use this environment
only when directed to do so by support personnel.

c11-01%
```

To leave the systemshell, type **exit**.

The root volume (vol0) is mounted on /mroot. The only way to directly access vol0 and its files is via the systemshell. Important subdirectories of vol0:

Pathname	contents
/mroot/etc/log and /mroot/etc/log/mlog	Logfiles
/mroot/etc/cluster_config/rdb	Replicated databases
/mroot/etc/backups/config	configuration backups

No matter how interesting the systemshell may be to many, this book will focus on the clustershell, since this is the shell for day to day administration and configuration.

Module 2 TRY THIS.

```
1. Connect to the administrative ip-address of cluster cl1.

What does you prompt look like?
Should be something like: cl1::>

What is the ONTAP version?

2. Press the <tab> key.

What happens?

3. Press the <?> key.

What happens?

4. Type "net" and press <enter>.

What happens?

5. Type "top" and press <enter>

What happens?

6. Type "set d" and press <enter>

What happens?

7. Type "systemshell" and press <tab>

What happens?

If you did not set this password yet, what do you have to do to set it and
successfully login to the systemshell?

8. Type "node run -node" and press <tab>

What happens?

9. Type "set admin" and press <enter>
   Type "man systemshell" and press <enter>

What happens?

10. Type "set d" and press <enter>
    Type "man systemshell"

What happens?
```

11. Type "cluster show" and press <enter>

What happens?

12. Type "cluster show -fields health" and press <enter>

What happens?

3. Disks, Raidgroups and Aggregates.

3.1 Aggregates.

An aggregate is a group of disks that belong together. An aggregate is always logically connected to one node at a time, but can failover to the other node in the HA-Pair if needed. The root aggregates as well as data aggregates can failover. Aggregates can be collections of harddisk drives, collections of harddisk drives in combination with SSDs, or you can have an environment where you only use SSDs. These environments are called All-Flash Arrays. All-Flash is the future, but since we are still in the present we also discuss regular, old fashioned aggregates. Conceptually, aggregates are aggregates, whether you use SSDs or not.

To view all aggregates in a cluster, the node that each aggregate is hosted by and the available size in each aggregate:

```
cl1::*> aggr show -fields nodes,availsize
aggregate node    availsize
--------- ------  ---------
aggr0_n1  cl1-01  661.4MB
aggr0_n2  cl1-02  661.4MB
n1_aggr1  cl1-01  49.11GB
n2_aggr1  cl1-02  49.22GB
4 entries were displayed.
```

The maximum size and the maximum number of disks per aggregate may vary per controller environment.

3.2 Raidgroups and Plexes.

Redundancy at the aggregate level is realized by creating raid groups in a Plex. In a default configuration the plex is named Plex0 and it is the only plex in the aggregate. In other words: an aggregate has a minimum of one plex and this plex is a collection of raidgroups. When a product called 'syncmirror' is used, the plex in an aggregate is mirrored with a second plex in the same aggregate. This is typically the case when you run a MetroCluster solution, which is not further dealt with in this book. Redundancy is of the type Raid4, Raid-DP or Raid-Tec which means that – per raid group – 1 , 2 or 3 disks respectively can fail at the same time without losing the data in the aggregate.

Raid type	Parity disks
Raid4	1
Raid-DP (dual parity)	2
Raid-Tec (triple erasure coding)	3

To view the raid types, the raid groups and the maximum raid group sizes:

```
cl1::*> aggr show -fields raidtype,raidgroups,maxraidsize
aggregate maxraidsize raidgroups                      raidtype
--------- ----------- --------------------------- --------
aggr0_n1  16          "/aggr0_n1/plex0/rg0 (block)" raid_dp
aggr0_n2  16          "/aggr0_n2/plex0/rg0 (block)" raid_dp
n1_aggr1  16          "/n1_aggr1/plex0/rg0 (block)"
                      "/n1_aggr1/plex0/rg1 (block)" raid_dp
n2_aggr1  16          "/n2_aggr1/plex0/rg0 (block)" raid_dp
4 entries were displayed.
```

Raid group sizes and raid types can be changed at the aggregate level.

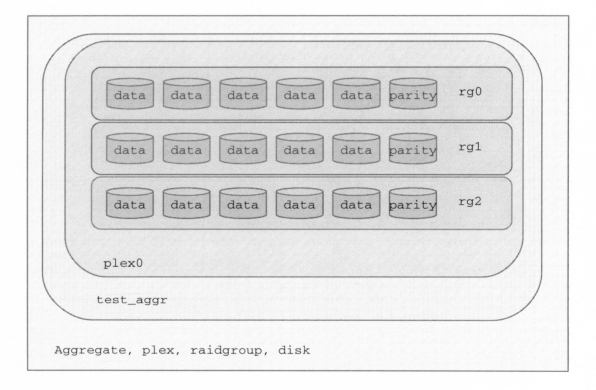

3.3 Disks.

Newly added disks to an HA-Pair, are unowned. This means that the disks are not assigned to any of the two controllers in the HA-Pair. By default, disk Auto Assign is on. So, after ten minutes, newly added disks are assigned to a controller based on the way the disk is cabled to the two controllers.

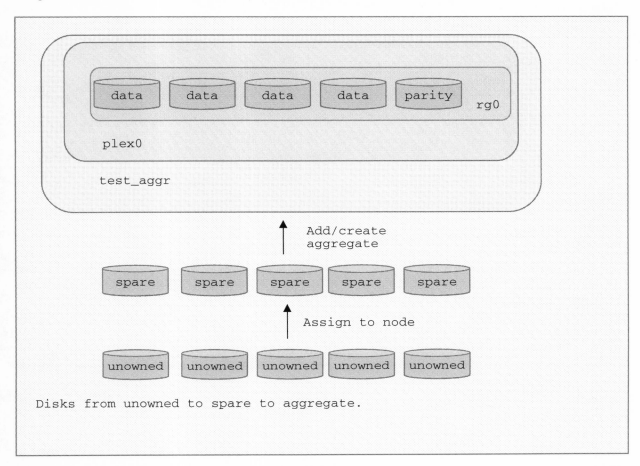

Disks that are assigned to a controller change from *unowned* to *spare*. Spare disks can be used to grow aggregates or to create new aggregates. Spare disks are also used when an aggregate disk fails. Per controller you should make sure to have some spare disks for every type and size of disks in use. Not having spare disks may result on your controller shutting down when aggregate disks fail.

The following disk container types are available:

Aggregate	Broken	Foreign	Labelmaint	Maintenance	Shared
Spare	Unassigned	Unknown	Unsupported	Remote	Mediator

To list disks of a particular container-type, run disk show -container-type <type>,<...>

```
cl1::*> disk show -container-type aggregate,spare
                 Usable             Disk   Container    Container
Disk             Size Shelf Bay     Type   Type         Name        Owner
--------------- ---------- ----- --- ------- ----------- --------- ---------

NET-1.1          3.93GB      -  24 FCAL    aggregate    n1_aggr1    cl1-01
NET-1.2          3.93GB      -  25 FCAL    spare        Pool0       cl1-01
NET-1.3          3.93GB      -  26 FCAL    spare        Pool0       cl1-01
NET-1.4          3.93GB      -  27 FCAL    spare        Pool0       cl1-01
NET-1.5          3.93GB      -  28 FCAL    spare        Pool0       cl1-01
NET-1.6          3.93GB      -  29 FCAL    spare        Pool0       cl1-01
NET-1.7          3.93GB      -  32 FCAL    spare        Pool0       cl1-01
NET-1.8          3.93GB      -  16 FCAL    aggregate    n1_aggr1    cl1-01
NET-1.9          3.93GB      -  17 FCAL    aggregate    n1_aggr1    cl1-01
NET-1.10         3.93GB      -  18 FCAL    aggregate    n1_aggr1    cl1-01
(output skipped)
```

3.4 Aggregates and available space.

Over time, aggregates may run out of space. An aggregate running out of space will need more raidgroups, or data has to be moved from one aggregate to another aggregate to free up space. It is important to realize that you can add disks to an aggregate but you cannot take them out again. The only way to free disks from an aggregate is by deleting the aggregate, which means you will have to delete the volumes first. Deleting volumes will result in losing data.

Therefore, an important decisionpoint is the time when you add disks to an aggregate, for it is irreversible. You can assign and re-assign disks at any time, until they are part of an aggregate.

Growing an aggregate is typically done before the aggregate is full. A (nearly) filled up aggregate will have no or little space left in its raidgroups. Adding a new raid group will make this raidgroup a potential hotspot for writes which will impact performance. It is advised to grow an aggregate that passes the 80% capacity threshold.

To view aggregate space, an example.

```
cl1::> aggr show -fields percent-used -aggregate n1_aggr1,n1_aggr2
aggregate percent-used
--------- ------------
n1_aggr1  2%
n1_aggr2  83%
2 entries were displayed.
```

Aggregate n1_aggr2 is filling up. You can move volumes to n1_aggr1, or you can grow the aggregate. NetApp's best practice for growing aggregates is to add raidgroups that hold more than half of the raidgroupsize. To view the raidgroupsize of an aggregate.

```
cl1::> aggr show -aggregate n1_aggr2 -fields maxraidsize
aggregate maxraidsize
--------- -----------
n1_aggr2  16
```

To grow this aggregate it is best practice to grow this aggregate with a raidgroup of 16. In our example we grow it by 10 disks, because we have no more disks available.

```
cl1::> aggr add -aggregate n1_aggr2 -diskcount 10
```

To view the space improvement:

```
cl1::> aggr show -fields percent-used -aggregate n1_aggr1,n1_aggr2
aggregate percent-used
--------- ------------
n1_aggr1  2%
n1_aggr2  46%
```

The next time you add disks to this aggregate, take into account that the 10 disk raidgroup will be filled out to 16 before a new raidgroup is created. It is obvious that adding disks is best done in raidgroupsize amounts.

When adding disks to the HA-Pair, the disks will have to be assigned, before they can be added to an aggregate. As stated earlier, disks are assigned automatically after ten minutes. Auto-assign can be switched to off and the auto-assign policy can be set to a *stack*, *shelf* or *bay*. The default setting depends on the controller type. Non-entry-level controllers and single node clusters default to stack, whereas entry-level systems default to bay.

```
Show autoassign-policy.
cl1::> disk option show -node c11-01,c11-02 -fields autoassign-policy
node    autoassign-policy
------  -----------------
cl1-01  shelf
cl1-02  default

Disable autoassign.
cl1::> disk option modify -node c11-01 -autoassign off
```

3.5 FlashPools.

To improve performance you can add SSD's to aggregates with harddisk drives. An aggregate that has one or more SSD raidgroups, offers better performance for random reads and random writes. FlashPools are sometimes called Hybrid pools. As with harddisk drives, once an SSD is added to the aggregate, it cannot be removed.

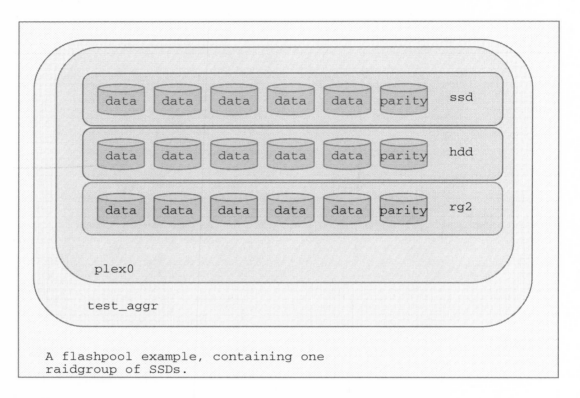

A flashpool example, containing one
raidgroup of SSDs.

3.5.1 Flash Pool considerations.

SSD stripes added to a Flash Pool do not contribute to the size of the aggregate.
Flash Pools are not supported with Array Luns (FlexArray)
Snapmirror destination volumes are not cached

3.5.2 Creating a Flash Pool.

To create a Flash Pool, first set hybrid-enabled to true, then add SSDs.

```
1. Change to hybrid.
c11::> aggr modify -aggregate n2_aggr1 -hybrid-enabled true

2. List SSDs.
c12::> disk show -type ssd
                      Usable              Disk    Container   Container
Disk                    Size Shelf Bay    Type    Type        Name      Owner
----------------   ---------- ----- ---   ------  ----------- --------- ---------
--------
NET-1.57             107.1MB     -   33   SSD     spare       Pool0     c12-01
NET-1.58             107.1MB     -   34   SSD     spare       Pool0     c12-01
NET-1.59             107.1MB     -   35   SSD     spare       Pool0     c12-01
NET-1.60             107.1MB     -   36   SSD     spare       Pool0     c12-01
NET-1.61             107.1MB     -   37   SSD     spare       Pool0     c12-01
NET-1.62             107.1MB     -   38   SSD     spare       Pool0     c12-01
(output skipped)

3. Add SSD raidgroup.
c12::> aggr add -aggregate aggr1 -diskcount 12 -disktype SSD
```

To check the result you can run aggr status from the node-shell to list the raidgroups and the disks.

```
c12::> node run -node c12-01 -command aggr status -r aggr1
Aggregate aggr1 (online, raid_dp, hybrid) (block checksums)
   Plex /aggr1/plex0 (online, normal, active, pool0)
     RAID group /aggr1/plex0/rg0 (normal, block checksums)

        RAID Disk    Device    HA   SHELF BAY CHAN Pool Type  RPM  Used
        ------------------------------------------------------------------------
        dparity      v0.19 v0    -    -     FC:A  0  FCAL 15000 4020/8233984
        parity       v0.20 v0    -    -     FC:A  0  FCAL 15000 4020/8233984
        data         v0.21 v0    -    -     FC:A  0  FCAL 15000 4020/8233984
        data         v0.22 v0    -    -     FC:A  0  FCAL 15000 4020/8233984
        data         v0.24 v0    -    -     FC:A  0  FCAL 15000 4020/8233984
        data         v0.25 v0    -    -     FC:A  0  FCAL 15000 4020/8233984

     RAID group /aggr1/plex0/rg1 (normal, block checksums)

        RAID Disk    Device    HA   SHELF BAY CHAN Pool Type  RPM  Used

        ------------------------------------------------------------------------
        dparity      v0.33     v0    -    -    SA:A  0  SSD  N/A 107/219264
        parity       v0.34     v0    -    -    SA:A  0  SSD  N/A 107/219264
        data         v0.35     v0    -    -    SA:A  0  SSD  N/A 107/219264
        data         v0.36     v0    -    -    SA:A  0  SSD  N/A 107/219264
        data         v0.37     v0    -    -    SA:A  0  SSD  N/A 107/219264
        data         v0.38     v0    -    -    SA:A  0  SSD  N/A 107/219264
        data         v0.39     v0    -    -    SA:A  0  SSD  N/A 107/219264
```

3.5.3 Storage Pools.

It is common knowledge that wider raidgroups give better performance. For resilience purposes the raidgroups are kept to a smaller than max default size. For SSDs the same holds true. Wider SSD raidgroups offer better performance. To offer wider stripes to separate nodes in a HA-PAIR, ONTAP can configure Storage Pools in which the SSDs are partitioned in four equal partitions and grouped together in allocation units. An allocation unit can be assigned to a node. This way you can have wider raidgroups than if you would assign complete SSDs to a node; both nodes in the HA-PAIR can now have wider stripes.

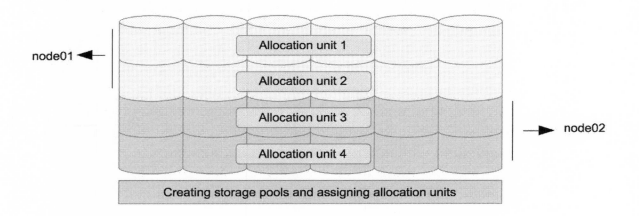

Create a storage pool and reassign allocation units.

```
Create a storage pool for the two nodes in the HA-PAIR.
cl1::*> storage pool create -storage-pool hybrid_pool1 -nodes cl1-01,cl1-02
-disk-count 8

Reassign an allocation unit from one node to another.
cl1::*> storage pool reassign -storage-pool hybrid_pool1 -from-node cl1-
01 -to-node cl1-02 -allocation-units 1
```

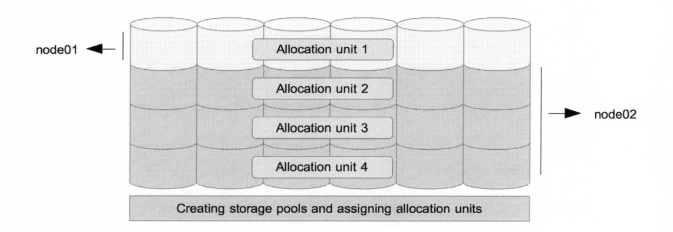

Module 3 TRY THIS.

1. *Connect to the administrative ip-address of cluster cl1.*

2. *List the available space in all aggregates in the cluster.*

3. *List all spare disks of node1.*

4. *Create an aggregate "test_aggr" with a diskcount and maxraidsize of six.*

5. *List the parity and data disks in aggregate test_aggr.*

6. *Are any SSD's available in your configuration?*

7. *list all available disktypes in your configuration.*

8. *Bring the aggregate test_aggr offline.*

9. *list all aggregates that are offline.*

10. *Bring the aggregate test_aggr online.*

11. Change the raidgroupsize to 8.

12. Add 8 disks to aggregate test_aggr.

13. How many disks are in raidgroup rg0 and how many are in rg1?

4. Storage Virtual Machines.

The Storage Virtual Machine (SVM), as discussed in module 1, is a container that houses volumes, logical interfaces and protocols. An SVM is not bound to a node and thus cannot be moved to a node. The volumes and logical interfaces can be migrated to other physical locations, though. When you create an SVM, its being there will be stored in the Management RDB on all nodes in the cluster. SVMs allow you to separate different types of data, and they offer the possibility to facilitate secure multi-tenancy if asked for. Mainly of this secure multi-tenancy, an SVM is always bound to an ipspace.

When you create an SVM, it will get a name, a root volume in an aggregate and a security-style. After creation you can add volumes and logical interfaces. The SVM also gets a type. Possible types are: *default* and dp-*destination*. The dp-destination type is for SVMDR, which will be discussed later.

To list the SVMs currently present, you use the **vserver show** command.

```
cl1::> vserver show
                                   Admin      Operational Root
Vserver        Type    Subtype    State      State       Volume     Aggregate
-----------    ------  ---------  ---------  ----------- ---------- ----------
cl1            admin   -          -          -           -          -
cl1-01         node    -          -          -           -          -
cl1-02         node    -          -          -           -          -
v_cifs         data    default    running    running     rv         n1_aggr1
v_iscsi        data    default    running    running     rv         n1_aggr1
v_nfs          data    default    running    running     rv         n1_aggr1
6 entries were displayed.
```

In the above example, you see the different types of SVMs possible: *admin*, *node* and *data*. Every node is an SVM. And there is an administrative vserver the ip address of which you use to login to the clustershell. The state of a data SVM can be *running* or *stopped*.

To view all properties of an SVM you use the **-instance** *argument* or specify the specific SVM.

```
cl1::> vserver show -vserver v_nfs
                               Vserver: v_nfs
                          Vserver Type: data
                       Vserver Subtype: default
                          Vserver UUID: 62ccd50b-2bf6-11e7-b2d1-
005056966a5a
                           Root Volume: rv
                             Aggregate: n1_aggr1
                            NIS Domain: -
            Root Volume Security Style: unix
                           LDAP Client: -
          Default Volume Language Code: C.UTF-8
                       Snapshot Policy: default
                               Comment:
                          Quota Policy: default
           List of Aggregates Assigned: -
 Limit on Maximum Number of Volumes allowed: unlimited
                   Vserver Admin State: running
             Vserver Operational State: running
     Vserver Operational State Stopped Reason: -
                     Allowed Protocols: nfs, cifs, fcp, iscsi, ndmp
                  Disallowed Protocols: -
(output skipped)
```

4.1 SVM creation.

To create an SVM you run the **vserver create** command.

```
cl1::> vserver create -vserver v_example -subtype default -rootvolume rv
-aggregate n1_aggr1 -rootvolume-security-style unix
[Job 105] Job succeeded:
Vserver creation completed
```

4.2 Adding volumes.

Volumes added to the namespace can be thin provisioned or thick provisioned. The difference is that a thin provisioned volume does not get the reserved space in the aggregate that it would get if it were thick provisioned. Thin provisioning is NetApp's current best practice. To create a thin provisioned volume you use the **-space-guarantee none** argument at creation time. The default value is **-space-guarantee volume**. If you want the volume to be accessible you have to specify a *junction-path*, or mount the volume afterwards. The junction-path is the directory in the namespace to which the volume is mounted. It is created automatically at mount time, and removed automatically when the volume is unmounted. Volumes can only be created in data SVMs.

To add a volume you run the **vol create** command.

```
cl1::> vol create -vserver v_example -volume examplevol -aggregate n1_aggr1
-size 500m -junction-path /ex_vol

Warning: The export-policy "default" has no rules in it. The volume will
therefore be inaccessible.
Do you want to continue? {y|n}: y
[Job 106] Job succeeded: Successful
```

To view the namespace of the SVM use the **vol show** command

```
cl1::> vol show -vserver v_example -fields junction-path
vserver     volume      junction-path
---------  ----------  -------------
v_example examplevol /ex_vol
v_example rv          /
2 entries were displayed.
```

4.3 Managing volumes.

We will discuss the following volume management options: *resizing, renaming, moving, unmounting, offlining* and *deleting*.

4.3.1. Volume resize.

A volume can be resized manually or automatically. To manually resize a volume use the **vol size** command.

```
cl1::> vol size -vserver v_example -volume examplevol -new-size 1g
vol size: Volume "v_example:examplevol" size set to 1g.
```

4.3.2 Automatic resize.

A volume can be automatically grown or shrunk based on the following parameters:

Mode	off grow grow_shrink
Trigger percentage	autosize-grow-threshold-percent autosize-shrink-threshold-percent

In the following example, the v_example volume will grow when its capacity reaches 85%.

```
cl1::*> vol modify -vserver v_example -volume examplevol -autosize-mode
grow -autosize-grow-threshold-percent 85%
```

4.3.3 Renaming a volume.

A volume can be renamed at any time. The volume does not have to be unmounted.

```
cl1::*> vol rename -vserver v_example -volume examplevol -newname ex_vol
```

4.3.4 Unmounting a volume.

Unmounting a volume will make the volume inaccessible for NAS clients. Also it will remove the junction-path of the volume. Mounting the volume will automatically create the junction-path.

```
cl1::*> vol unmount -vserver v_example -volume ex_vol
```

4.3.5 Removing a volume.

To remove a volume it should not be mounted and it should be offline.

```
cl1::*> vol offline -vserver v_example -volume ex_vol
Volume "v_example:ex_vol" is now offline.

cl1::*> vol delete -vserver v_example -volume ex_vol

Warning: Are you sure you want to delete volume "ex_vol" in Vserver
"v_example" ? {y|n}: y
[Job 109] Job succeeded: Successful
```

By default a volume can be recovered for 12 hours before it is permanently removed. To reduce that time, modify the vserver property **volume-delete-retention-hours**.

To manually remove a volume that is in the recovery queue, use the **purge** argument. To recover it, use the recover argument. In the following example, we delete a volume, and see that the type changes to *DEL*. Then we purge the volume.

```
cl1::*> vol offline -vserver v_example -volume v_two
Volume "v_example:v_two" is now offline.

cl1::*> vol delete -vserver v_example -volume v_two

Warning: Are you sure you want to delete volume "v_two" in Vserver
"v_example" ? {y|n}: y

cl1::*> vol show -vserver v_example -volume
    rv          v_two_1034
cl1::*> vol show -vserver v_example
Vserver    Volume       Aggregate    State      Type      Size  Available Used
%
---------- ------------ ---------- ---------- ---- ---------- ----------
-----
v_example rv            n1_aggr1  online     RW          20MB    18.76MB
6%
v_example v_two_1034    n1_aggr1  offline    DEL        100MB           -
-
2 entries were displayed.

cl1::*> vol recovery-queue purge -vserver v_example -volume ex_vol_1033
```

4.3.6 Moving a volume.

You may want to move a volume, to spread the load or to free up space in an aggregate. Moving a volume is transparent to clients that use the volume. Moving a volumes invokes a snapmirror relationship that will replicate the volume to another aggregate and will eventually remove the original volume.

In the following example we move volume 'nas_volume' from its current aggregate n1_aggr1 to n2_aggr1.

```
1. Determine current aggregate.
cl1::> vol show -vserver nas_svm -volume nas_volume -fields aggregate
vserver volume       aggregate
------- ----------   ---------
nas_svm nas_volume   n1_aggr1

2. Move the volume.
cl1::> vol move start -vserver nas_svm -volume nas_volume -destination-
aggregate n2_aggr1

3. Determine current aggregate.
cl1::> vol show -vserver nas_svm -volume nas_volume -fields aggregate
vserver volume       aggregate
------- ----------   ---------
nas_svm nas_volume   n2_aggr1
```

4.3.7 Rehosting a volume.

Moving a volume to a another SVM does not move the volume data. It only *rehosts* the volume to the destination SVM. The volume should be unmounted before rehosting it, or the action will fail.

```
1. Unmount the volume.
cl1::> vol unmount -vserver nas_svm -volume nas_volume

2. Rehost the volume.
cl1::> vol rehost -vserver nas_svm -volume nas_volume -destination-vserver
v_iscsi
```

Rehosting a volume can be handy if you have set it up in a test environment and now want to move it to production.

4.4 SVM deletion.

To delete an SVM all volumes should be removed, including the rootvolume. The SVM should not be in any sort of relationship like snapmirror or peering (discussed later).

```
cl1::*> vol offline -vserver v_example rv

Warning: Offlining root volume rv of Vserver v_example will make all
volumes on that Vserver inaccessible.
Do you want to continue? {y|n}: y
Volume "v_example:rv" is now offline.

cl1::*> vol delete -vserver v_example -volume rv

Warning: Are you sure you want to delete volume "rv" in Vserver "v_example"
? {y|n}: y
[Job 111] Job succeeded: Successful

cl1::*> vserver delete -vserver v_example
```

Module 4 TRY THIS.

1. List all Storage Virtual Machines.

2. Create a new SVM called 'testvserver' with a rootvolume called 'rv' and a rootvolume security style 'unix'.

3. Create a 100MB volume called 'datavol' in the testvserver and mount it to
   a junction-path with the same name.

4. Resize the new volume to 200MB.

5. Create a thin provisioned volume called 'thin' in testvserver of 200MB
   and mount it to the 'thin' junction-path.

6. Create a second SVM and move the volume datavol to the new SVM.

7. Move the volume 'datavol' to another aggregate.

8. Delete the volume 'datavol'.

9. What is the delete-retention time for volumes in the SVM 'testsvm'?

10. Remove the volume 'datavol' permanently and set the retention time to 0

11. Delete the SVM testsvm

5. Networking.

ONTAP has four different types of networks:

Type	Configurable	Function
HA-Interconnect	No	NVRAM-mirroring
Cluster-Interconnect	Yes	Heartbeat, configuration, replication, volume data
Management	Yes	Cluster and node management
Data	Yes	Client data traffic

5.1 HA-Interconnect.

The nodes are usually connected via the backplane of the chassis. If not, then two ports on both nodes are used to cable (c0a, c0b). The HA-Interconnect is primarily used for NVRAM-mirroring. This network does not show up in the network information in the clustershell. The administrator does not manage this network.

5.2 Cluster Interconnect.

Each node has a minimum of two 10Gb interfaces, these are either cabled point-to-point to the other node in the HA-Pair, or a switched network is used. In that case you can easily scale out by adding more HA-Pairs to to cluster. The network shows up from the clustershell and is configured during cluster setup.
  If you decide to start with a single node cluster, you can manually add this network if you want to scale-out. More interfaces can be added for more bandwidth and better performance. This is usually not necessary.

In the following example the net int show command displays the Cluster vserver that has the cluster interconnect lifs on physical ports e0a and e0b, two ports per node.

```
cl1::> net int show
   (network interface show)
            Logical      Status    Network              Current  Current  Is
Vserver   Interface   Admin/Oper Address/Mask          Node     Port     Home
--------- ----------- ---------- -------------------- -------------- -------- -------
Cluster
          cl1-01_clus1 up/up      169.254.106.90/16   cl1-01   e0a      true
          cl1-01_clus2 up/up      169.254.188.236/16  cl1-01   e0b      true
          cl1-02_clus1 up/up      169.254.167.212/16  cl1-02   e0a      true
          cl1-02_clus2 up/up      169.254.108.205/16  cl1-02   e0b      true

(output skipped)
```

To check the health of the Cluster Interconnect network, you can run the **cluster ping-cluster** command in the advanced mode.

In the example we see that connectivity is successful on all 4 paths.

```
cl1::*> cluster ping-cluster -node cl1-01
Host is cl1-01
Getting addresses from network interface table...
Cluster cl1-01_clus1 cl1-01    e0a        169.254.106.90
Cluster cl1-01_clus2 cl1-01    e0b        169.254.188.236
Cluster cl1-02_clus1 cl1-02    e0a        169.254.167.212
Cluster cl1-02_clus2 cl1-02    e0b        169.254.108.205
Local = 169.254.106.90 169.254.188.236
Remote = 169.254.167.212 169.254.108.205
Cluster Vserver Id = 4294967293
Ping status:
....
Basic connectivity succeeds on 4 path(s)
Basic connectivity fails on 0 path(s)
................
Detected 1500 byte MTU on 4 path(s):
    Local 169.254.106.90 to Remote 169.254.108.205
    Local 169.254.106.90 to Remote 169.254.167.212
    Local 169.254.188.236 to Remote 169.254.108.205
    Local 169.254.188.236 to Remote 169.254.167.212
Larger than PMTU communication succeeds on 4 path(s)
RPC status:
2 paths up, 0 paths down (tcp check)
2 paths up, 0 paths down (udp check)
```

To watch the live traffic you can use the **statistics** command.

```
cl1::*> statistics show-periodic -object lif -interval 2 -instance cl1-
01_clus1 -counter recv_data|sent_data
cl1: lif.cl1-01_clus1: 5/1/2017 09:02:54
    recv      sent
    data      data
 --------  --------
     862B    1.24KB
     637B     1020B
     603B     1014B
```

5.3 Management Network.

The cluster's management network has a physical port called e0M. The port is internally connected to a switch. Behind the switch there is a Service Processor (SP) and the regular e0M port for management. The SP gives access to the console of the node. So this port has two ip addresses. This is useful when you have to access the console from a remote site. The SP address can be configured from the clustershell.

```
cl1::> system node service-processor network modify -node node1
-address-type IPv4 -enable true -ip-address 192.168.123.98 -netmask
255.255.255.0 -gateway 192.168.123.1
```

You can setup the SP interactively with the following command

```
system node run -node <nodename> sp setup
```

A few important SP commands:

system battery	Battery related commands
system battery show	Displays the system battery status
system console	Toggles to the system console
system core	Dumps the system core and resets the filer
system log	Displays the system console logs on the console
system power	Command set for controlling system power
system power cycle	Toggles the system power off, then back on
system power off	Powers the system off
system power on	Powers the system on
system power status	Displays the system power status
system reset	Resets the system

5.4 Data Network.

Obviously the data network is for transporting data from volumes and luns to and from clients. The major configuration part is to be executed for this network. We will first make a division between physical, virtual and logical entities, and then we will talk about ipspaces, broadcast domains and subnets.

Every node in the cluster has physical ports that can be used for data traffic. These ports are network ports and fibrechannel ports. A third interface is the Unified Target Port (UTA) that can be configured either as an ethernet port or a fibre channel port.

To view your FC ports run the **fcadmin** command. The FC ports are named 0a/0b/0c/0d

```
node run -node node1 fcadmin config
Adapter Type       State            Status
0a    target     CONFIGURED         online
0b    target     CONFIGURED         online
0c    initiator  CONFIGURED         offline
0d    target     CONFIGURED         online
```

To view your ethernet ports run the **net port** command. The ethernet ports are named e0a/e0b/e0c/e0d.

```
cl1::> net port show
  (network port show)

Node: cl1-01
                                             Speed(Mbps) Health
Port      IPspace      Broadcast Domain Link MTU  Admin/Oper  Status
--------  -----------  ---------------- ---- ---- ----------- --------
e0a       Cluster      Cluster          up   1500 auto/1000   healthy
e0b       Cluster      Cluster          up   1500 auto/1000   healthy
e0c       Default      Default          up   1500 auto/1000   healthy
e0d       Default      Default          up   1500 auto/1000   healthy

Node: cl1-02
                                             Speed(Mbps) Health
Port      IPspace      Broadcast Domain Link MTU  Admin/Oper  Status
--------  -----------  ---------------- ---- ---- ----------- --------
e0a       Cluster      Cluster          up   1500 auto/1000   healthy
e0b       Cluster      Cluster          up   1500 auto/1000   healthy
e0c       Default      Default          up   1500 auto/1000   healthy
e0d       Default      Default          up   1500 auto/1000   healthy
8 entries were displayed.
```

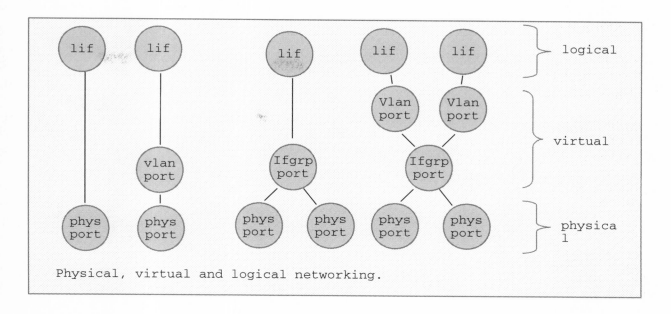

Physical, virtual and logical networking.

5.5 Virtual Ports.

Virtual ports are either interface group ports or vlan ports. Both types in the end have one or more physical ports at their base, but they will show up with the same **net port** command.

5.5.1 Interface Groups.

An interface group virtual port is a collection of physical ports. You can create an interface group in one of three modes: multi, single or LACP.

Multi-mode interface groups are partly compliant with IEEE 802.3ad. Multi-mode interface groups support static configuration but not dynamic aggregate creation. In a multi-mode interface group, all links are simultaneously active. This mode is only useful if all the links are connected to a switch that supports trunking/aggregation over multiple port connections. The switch must be configured to understand that all the port connections share a common media access control (MAC) address and are part of a single logical interface.

Dynamic multi-mode (LACP) interface groups are completely compliant with IEEE 802.3ad. LACP protocol is used determine which of the underlying links can be aggregated. LACP protocol is also used to monitor the link status. If the configuration on both ends of the links is correct, then all the interfaces of an interface group are active.5.5.2 VLANs.

5.5.2 VLAN Ports. Vlan Ports can be configured on physical port or interface group ports. VLANs provide logical segmentation of networks by creating separate broadcast domains. A VLAN can span multiple physical network segments. The end-stations belonging to a VLAN are related by function or application.

For example, end-stations in a VLAN might be grouped by departments, such as engineering and accounting, or by projects, such as project1 and project2. Because physical proximity of the end-stations is not essential in a VLAN, you can disperse the end-stations geographically and still contain the broadcast domain in a switched network.

In the following example, two physical ports are grouped in a0a with loadbalancing on ip address.

```
cl2::*> ifgrp create -node cl2-01 -ifgrp a0a -distr-func ip
-mode multimode_lacp
cl2::network port*> ifgrp add-port -node cl2-01 -ifgrp a0a -port e0a

cl2::network port*> ifgrp add-port -node cl2-01 -ifgrp a0a -port e0b

cl2::*> ifgrp show
          Port        Distribution                        Active
Node      IfGrp       Function      MAC Address           Ports    Ports
--------  ----------  ------------  -----------------     -------
cl2-01
          a0a         ip            02:50:56:96:a7:70 none    -
```

In the following example, two VLAN Ports are created on two different physical ports. These two ports are not redundant in themselves, but could together create a failover possibility for any LIF created on one of the ports.

```
cl1::> vlan create -node cl1-01 -vlan-name e0d-10
cl1::> vlan create -node cl1-02 -vlan-name e0d-10
cl1::> vlan show
                    Network Network
Node     VLAN Name  Port    VLAN ID  MAC Address
------   ---------  ------- -------- -----------------
cl1-01
         e0d-10     e0d     10       00:50:56:96:94:32
cl1-02
         e0d-10     e0d     10       00:50:56:96:a4:bc
2 entries were displayed.
```

5.6 Ipspaces and Broadcast domains, ports and lifs.

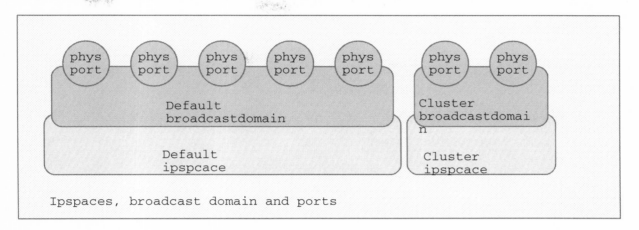

Ipspaces, broadcast domain and ports

An ipspace is a container for one or more broadcast domains. So, initially an ipspace is empty. Then, a broadcast domain should be added. This broadcast domain then will be populated with physical and or virtual ports.

```
cl2::*> ipspace create cust
cl2::*> broadcast-domain create -broadcast-domain cust -ipspace cust
cl2::*> broadcast-domain add-ports -broadcast-domain cust
-ports cl2-01:a0a -ipspace cust
```

The main reason for having multiple ipspaces is to facilitate secure multi-tenancy where customers are offered separate physical networks. They may have identical subnets. However, if you don't need separate ipspaces, then all ports that are not used for the cluster interconnect will be in the *default broadcast domain* in the *default ipspace*. The cluster interconnect ports are in the Cluster broadcast domain in the Cluster ipspace.

A broadcast domain is a collection of multiple ports from different nodes in the same cluster. You can have multiple broadcast domains in the same ipspace. One broadcast domain per ipspace is the minimum. Ports can be added to or removed from a broadcast domain. Physical ports that belong to an interface group, should not be in any broadcast-domain. The following example removes two ports from the Default broadcast-domain, creates an interface group of these two ports and adds the ifgrp **a0a** to the Default broadcast-domain.

```
cl1::> broadcast-domain remove-ports -broadcast-domain Default -ports cl1-
01:e0d
cl1::> broadcast-domain remove-ports -broadcast-domain Default -ports cl1-
01:e0c
cl1::*> ifgrp create -node cl1-01 -ifgrp a0a -distr-func ip -mode multimode
cl1::*> ifgrp add-port -node cl1-01 -ifgrp a0a -port e0c
cl1::*> ifgrp add-port -node cl1-01 -ifgrp a0a -port e0d
cl1::*> broadcast-domain add-ports -broadcast-domain Default -ports cl1-
01:a0a
```

5.6.1 SVMs and ipspaces.

Storage Virtual Machines are connected to an ipspace at creation. By default every SVM is connected to the Default ipspace. You cannot change the relationship once the SVM is set up. You can only remove the SVM and recreate it and link it to the correct ipspace.

The following SVM is linked to the cust ipspace.

```
C12::*> vserver create -vserver cust_svm -ipspace cust -subtype
default -rootvolume rv -aggregate aggr1 -rootvolume-security-style unix
```

The fact that SVMs are always connected to one particular ipspace is important to realize, because it automatically determines the ports that can be used to create ip-addresses for the SVM. For example: SVM-1 is created to ipspace OFFICE. Ports that to not belong to a broadcast domain in ipspace OFFICE, cannot be used to setup ip-addresses for SVM-1.

5.7 Subnets.

It is optional to create a subnet in the broadcast domain. Lifs will automatically get an ip address assigned at creation based on the subnet.

```
c12::*> subnet create -subnet-name cust_net -broadcast-domain cust -subnet
192.168.4.0/24 -ipspace cust -gateway 192.168.4.1 -ip-ranges 192.168.4.230-
192.168.4.235
    (network subnet create)
```

5.8 Logical Interfaces.

Logical Interfaces (Lifs) are always created in an SVM, like volumes. You can create multiple Lifs per SVM and multiple Lifs per port. By default NAS Lifs can failover to all ports in the broadcast domain. If this is not desired because you for example have a combination of Vlans and Physical port in the same broadcast domain, you can define failover-groups with a specific type of ports. The Lif can then be connected to a particular failover-group.

To limit the failover possibility to defined ports, we create a failover-group – a collection of ports in a broadcast domain – to which we connect the lif.

```
c11::> vserver create -vserver v_example -subtype default -rootvolume rv
-aggregate n1_aggr1 -rootvolume-security-style unix
[Job 127] Job succeeded:
Vserver creation completed

c11::> failover-group create -vserver v_example -failover-group fg_example
-targets c11-01:e0c
    (network interface failover-groups create)

c11::> failover-group add-targets -vserver v_example -failover-group
fg_example -targets c11-02:e0c
    (network interface failover-groups add-targets)
```

Now that the SVM and Failover-group are setup, we can create a lif for the SVM. The Lif will get an ip address, a netmask, a protocol, a role and a failover-group. We have connected this SVM to the Default ipspace, there is no subnet, so we will manually specify an ip address and netmask.

```
c11::> net int create -vserver v_example -lif ex_1 -role data -data-
protocol nfs -home-node c11-01 -home-port e0c -address 192.168.4.210
-netmask 255.255.255.0 -status-admin up -failover-group fg_example
    (network interface create)
```

A Lif can get one of the following roles:

Role	Description
cluster	Used for communication using the private cluster network
data	Used for communicating with file service clients
node-mgmt	Used by administrators to configure the node
intercluster	Used for communication with a different cluster
cluster-mgmt	Used by administrators to configure the cluster

An SVM can have Lifs with a particular role, depending on the SVM type.

SVM-type	Role	Network
system	cluster	Cluster-Interconnect
admin	node-mgmt cluster-mgmt intercluster	Management Management Intercluster
node	node-mgmt cluster intercluster	Management Cluster-Interconnect Intercluster
data	data	data

These two lists may seem confusing, but the choice of roles possible are limited by the type of SVM you are creating the Lif for. Most Lifs will be for SVMs of the type *data*, so the only possible role will be *data*.

5.9 Firewall-policies.

A firewall policy is a combination of allowed services and client ip's. The list of services you can choose from when setting up a new firewall policy or modifying an existing one:

dns	ndmp	ndmps	http	https
ntp	rsh	ssh	telnet	snmp

Firewall policies can be created and removed. Predefined firewall policies can be modified but they cannot be deleted.

5.9.1 Predefined firewall policies.

The predefined firewall policies include: **data**, **intercluster** and **mgmt**.

```
cl1::*> firewall policy  show
   (system services firewall policy show)
Vserver Policy          Service    Allowed
------- -------------   ---------------------------------
cl1
        data
                        dns        0.0.0.0/0
                        ndmp       0.0.0.0/0
                        ndmps      0.0.0.0/0
cl1
        intercluster
                        https      0.0.0.0/0
                        ndmp       0.0.0.0/0
                        ndmps      0.0.0.0/0
cl1
        mgmt
                        dns        0.0.0.0/0
                        http       0.0.0.0/0
                        https      0.0.0.0/0
                        ndmp       0.0.0.0/0
                        ndmps      0.0.0.0/0
```

Lifs in the *Cluster* SVM have no firewall policy. All other Lifs do have a firewall policy. Typically a firewall policy will *allow* for management or will *not allow* for management. Mind you, these firewall policies have no effect on the NAS and SAN protocols. They are only used to manage access of the services mentioned.

Confused? Here is an example:

The SVM **v_example** has a lif **ex_1**, that has firewall policy **data**. This means that this lif does not allow for *ssh* or any other management protocol. You decide that a customer should be able to login to the SVM with putty, plink or ssh. The firewall policy data does not allow that. You change the firewall policy for that particular Lif to mgmt. If you want to limit the clients that can access using ssh, you can create a policy in the SVM and allow ssh for the client.

```
cl1::*> firewall policy create -vserver v_example -policy ssh_only -service
ssh -allow-list 192.168.4.158/24

cl1::*> firewall policy show -vserver v_example -policy ssh_only
v_example
        ssh_only
                        ssh        192.168.4.158/24

cl1::*> net int modify -vserver v_example -lif ex_1 -firewall-policy
ssh_only

cl1::*> net int show -vserver v_example -lif ex_1 -fields firewall-policy
v_example ex_1 ssh_only
```

Module 5 TRY THIS.

1. *List all ports and their ipspace and broadcast-domain.*

2. *Create a logical interface in an existing SVM and make sure the LIF only supports NFS. The ip-address is '192.168.10.10', the netmask is '255.255.255.0'. The port is e0c on node1.*

3. *List the ipspace of every SVM.*

4. *Create a route entry for the SVM 'testsvm'.*

5. *Create a failover-group for SVM testsvm with the e0c ports of node1 and node2.*

6. *Connect the lif you created in 2. to the failover-group 'testgroup'.*

7. *Migrate the lif 'lif1' to port e0c on node2.*

8. *Revert the lif back to its home-node and home-port.*

9. *Change the home-node of the lif 'lif1' to node 2, and revert the lif.*

10. *Create a firewall policy that allows only ssh for all clients and connect the firewall policy to lif1.*

6. Peering.

SVMs can be peered for disaster recovery purposes or for backup and restore purposes. You can peer SVMS that live in the same cluster, but this is not common practice. Typically SVMs that live in different clusters are peered. This book will focus on SVMs that live in different clusters.

6.1 Cluster peering.

To peer two clusters, you need Lifs that allow for intercluster traffic. All of the intercluster LIFs of one cluster must be able to communicate with all of the intercluster LIFs of the cluster peer. This is referred to as *pair-wise full-mesh connectivity*.

6.2 Intercluster Lifs.

In the example, we setup up the two Lifs on cluster cl1 and the one Lif on cluster cl2. All three Lifs will get the *intercluster* role.

Cluster	Port	Node	Lif	Address
cl1	e0c	cl1-01	il1	192.168.10.1
cl1	e0c	cl1-01	il2	192.168.10.2
cl2	e0c	cl1-02	il1	192.168.10.3

```
cl1::*> net int create -vserver cl1 -lif il1 -role intercluster -home-node
cl1-01 -home-port e0c -address 192.168.10.1 -netmask 255.255.255.0 -status-
admin up
  (network interface create)

cl1::*> net int create -vserver cl1 -lif il2 -role intercluster -home-node
cl1-02 -home-port e0c -address 192.168.10.2 -netmask 255.255.255.0 -status-
admin up
  (network interface create)

cl2::*> net int create -vserver cl2 -lif il1 -role intercluster -home-node
cl2-01 -home-port e0c -address 192.168.10.3 -netmask 255.255.255.0 -status-
admin up
  (network interface create)
```

To check intercluster connectivity:

```
cl1::*> network ping -node cl1-01 -destination 192.168.10.3
192.168.10.3 is alive

cl2::*> network ping -node cl2-01 -destination 192.168.10.1
192.168.10.1 is alive

cl2::*> network ping -node cl2-01 -destination 192.168.10.2
192.168.10.2 is alive
```

6.3 Setup a cluster peer relationship.

Peering can be done with or without authentication. In this example we will not use authentication. The peer command will have to run on both clusters. The same passphrase should be used.

```
cl1::*> cluster peer show
This table is currently empty.

cl1::*> cluster peer create -peer-addrs 192.168.10.3

Notice: Choose a passphrase of 8 or more characters. To ensure the
authenticity of the peering relationship, use a phrase or
        sequence of characters that would be hard to guess.

Enter the passphrase: ********
Confirm the passphrase: ********

cl2::*> cluster peer create -peer-addrs 192.168.10.1

Notice: Choose a passphrase of 8 or more characters. To ensure the
authenticity of the peering relationship, use a phrase or sequence of
characters that
        would be hard to guess.

Enter the passphrase: ********
Confirm the passphrase: ********


cl1::*> cluster peer show
Peer Cluster Name Cluster Serial Number Availability   Authentication
----------------- --------------------- -------------- --------------
cl2                         1-80-000008  Available      ok
```

6.4 Setup SVM peering.

To setup SVM peering, the relationship needs to be setup from one SVM and accepted by the other. The order is irrelevant. Once the relationship is setup, it works both ways. Also, the relationship needs an application that is supported in the relationship.

6.4.1 Supported applications.

The following applications are supported:

snapmirror	Snapmirror
file-copy	Filecopy
lun-copy	Luncopy

A comma-separated list of supported applications can be specified and these can be modified afterwards.

6.4.2 Setup the SVM peer relation.

In this example we will create two SVMs – in already peered clusters – and peer them with support for snapmirror.

```
cl1::*> vserver peer create -vserver v_cl1 -peer-vserver v_cl2
-applications snapmirror -peer-cluster cl2

cl2::*> vserver peer show
Peer       Peer        Peering      Remote
Vserver    Vserver     State        Peer Cluster  Applications Vserver
---------- ----------- ------------ ------------- ------------ --------
v_cl2      v_cl1       pending      cl1                        snapmirror   v_cl1

cl2::*> vserver peer accept -vserver v_cl2 -peer-vserver v_cl1

cl2::*> vserver peer show
Peer       Peer        Peering    Remote
Vserver    Vserver     State      Peer Cluster Applications   Vserver
---------- ---------   --------   ------------ ------------   -------
v_cl2      v_cl1       peered     cl1                        snapmirror   v_cl1
```

6.5 Delete peering relationships.

To delete peering of the SVM and of the cluster, reverse the order. First delete SVM peering and then cluster peering. In this case, no applications have been set up yet, so deletion is easy. If applications were assigned you would have to get rid of these applications first.

```
cl1::*> vserver peer delete -vserver v_cl1 -peer-vserver v_cl2

cl1::*> cluster peer delete -cluster cl2

cl2::*> cluster peer delete -cluster cl1
```

Module 6 TRY THIS.

1. Create two SVMs, 'srcsvm' and dstsvm, with rootvolume 'rv', aggregate 'n1_aggr' and rootvolume security style 'unix'.

2. Peer the two SVMs for the application 'snapmirror'.

3. Suspend the peer relation between the two SVMs.

4. Resume the peer relation.

5. Delete the two SVMs.

7. WAFL

NetApp's Write Anywhere File Layout (WAFL) is often referred to as a file system. But actually, it is more than a file system. A file system takes care of maintaining a structured order of inodes and blocks that are represented to us as a hierarchical collection of files and folders. WAFL also takes care of the physical disks by arranging them in pools with a redundancy type. So WAFL also functions as a volume manager. You could say that WAFL has a *logical* layer that takes care of the file system and a *physical* layer that takes care of the aggregates and raidgroups. This module concentrates on the logical layer.

7.1 Inodes.

A WAFL inode is 192 bytes in size, has a unique number in the file system, and holds the properties of a file. You should think of: *the size of a file*, *the type of file*, *the permissions of a file*, *ownership information* and *timestamp of last access*, *last change-* and *last modificationtimestamp* of the inode. A quick example:

On a Linux/UNIX client, running the `ls -l` command, will give you this information.

```
root# ls -li file1
670689 -rw-r--r-- 1 pi pi 6 Jul  4 15:23 file1
```

In the above example we see the following properties:

Inode	Type	Permissions	Linkcount	Userid	Groupid	Size 6 bytes	Changedate
670689	–	rw-r--r--	1	pi	pi		Jul 4 15:23

Next to file properties, the inode also contains pointers to data blocks and pointers to blocks that hold more pointers. At the top of the file system inode blocks and data blocks there is one inode that is called the root inode. The logical block size of WAFL blocks is 4KB.

Representation of the WAFL structure:

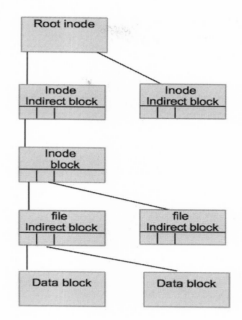

Inodes contain the properties of a file plus pointers to datablocks. Indirect blocks contain pointers only. Datablocks contain file-data.

7.2 Consistency point.

In module 1 paragraph 1.15 we discussed the consistency point briefly. A consistency point means that a new root inode is written. All data blocks and in between blocks are written first, from the bottom up. WAFL never overwrites an active block. So, in the graphical example, when the contents of a data block is changed by the client, a new data block is written, then a new file indirect block, a new inode block, a new inode indirect block and finally, the new root inode is written. Once the new root inode is in place, a new view of the active filesystem is a fact and NVRAM can be flushed.

Remember, when an aggregate is created, WAFL creates the aggregate file system, including a root inode. Every data volume in the aggregate has its own root inode inside the aggregate filesystem. The root inode of a volume can be seen as an administrative starting point for a hierarchical structure of inode blocks and data blocks, within that particular volume.

7.3 Snapshot.

A snapshot is a point in time copy of a file system and it is always read only. This copy is realized by copying the root inode of the active filesystem of the aggregate or of the volume. Typically, volume snapshots are created instead of aggregate snapshots.[1]

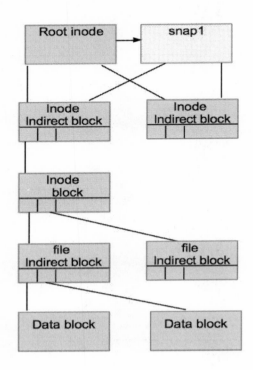

Snapshots are used to restore accidentally removed files. They are also used to replicate blocks to another volume, for disaster recovery purposes or for backup purposes. The maximum number of snapshots per volume is 1023[2].

Snapshots can also be used as parent for FlexClone volumes (7.3.4).

---

1   Aggregate snapshots are used in Metro Cluster.
2   This depends on the ONTAP version.

7.3.1 Creating snapshots.

```
cl1::> vol create -vserver v_example -volume exvol -aggregate n1_aggr1
-size 500m -junction-path /exvol

cl1::> snap create -vserver v_example -volume exvol -snapshot exsnap1
```

You can have an absolute maximum of 1023 snapshots per volume. As we have seen in the example, snapshots can be created manually. They can also be schedule by creating a snapshot policy. In the following example we create a snapshot policy with a schedule of 5 minutes, a retention of two snapshots and a prefix of 'example_'. And we connect the snapshot policy to a volume in the namespace.

```
cl1::> snapshot policy create -policy examplepol -enabled true -schedule1
5min -count1 2 -prefix1 example_ -vserver v_example

cl1::> vol modify -vserver v_example -volume exvol -snapshot-policy
examplepol
```

Note: by default when creating a volume, the volume will get the default policy which maintains 6 hourly, 2 daily and 2 weekly snapshots. You should not create or keep unnecessary snapshots because, initially they do not take any space, but as the active filesystem changes, snapshots will keep blocks locked and thus claim space.

7.3.2 Restoring snapshots.

There are multiple ways to restore accidentally removed files or to restore an entire volume.

1. Restore snapshot
2. Restore single file.
3. Use a NAS client to access the snapshot directory and copy files back to the active filesystem.

In the following example a snapshot will be restored. First all snapshots for a volume are listed. You see that there is one snapshot, it uses 8% of the total volume space and 94% of the blocks are in the snapshot.

It is important to realize that a snap restore cannot be made undone. Also keep in mind, that when you restore a snapshot, all snapshots that were created after that snapshot, will be gone because they were not there when the restored snapshot was created. Restoring single files as in option 2 and 3, does not remove any snapshots.

```
cl1::> snap show -vserver v_example -volume exvol


---Blocks---
Vserver  Volume   Snapshot                         Size Total% Used%
-------- -------- ------------------------- -------- ------ -----
v_example
         exvol
                  example.2017-05-04_0700   38.28MB     8%    94%


cl1::> snap restore -vserver v_example -volume exvol -snapshot
example.2017-05-04_0700
```

In the next example, a single file – kernel.img – is restored from an available snapshot. Then the same file is restored under a different name.

```
cl1::> snap restore-file -vserver v_example -volume exvol -snapshot
example.2017-05-04_0710 -path /kernel.img

cl1::> snap restore-file -vserver v_example -volume exvol -r
/kernelrestore.img -snapshot example.2017-05-04_0715 -path /kernel.img
```

To access the volume from an NFS client, you will have to create an export-policy, connect the policy to the volume, the root volume and enable NFS in the SVM. The SVM needs an ip address. Then you can connect from an NFS client to the volume and access the .snapshot directory.

```
cl1::> export-policy create -vserver v_example -policyname ex_pol

cl1::> export-policy rule create -policyname ex_pol -vserver v_example
-clientmatch 0.0.0.0/0 -rorule any -rwrule any -superuser any

cl1::> vol modify -vserver v_example  -volume exvol -policy ex_pol
cl1::> vol modify -vserver v_example  -volume rv -policy ex_pol


cl1::> nfs on v_example

cl1::> net int create -vserver v_example -lif l1 -role data -data-protocol
nfs -home-node cl1-01 -home-port e0d -address 192.168.4.222 -netmask
255.255.255.0

root:~# mkdir /mnt/222
root:~# mount 192.168.4.222:/exvol /mnt/222
```

Note: setting up NFS will be discussed in a later module.

Now you can access the .snapshot directory from the client and restore any file from any snapshot back to the active filesystem, by copying it.

```
root:/mnt/222# cd /mnt/222/.snapshot

root:/mnt/222/.snapshot# ls
example.2017-05-04_0725   example.2017-05-04_0730

root:/mnt/222/.snapshot# cd example.2017-05-04_0725

root:/mnt/222/.snapshot/example.2017-05-04_0725# cp kernel.img /mnt/222/
```

Copying a file to the active filesystem is not the same as restoring a pointer. Copying a file does take additional space

7.3.3 Snapshot reserve.

By default, 5% of a volume is reserved for snapshots. This means that, for example, a 10GB volume will have a snapshot reserve of 500MB. This means that the available space in the volume is 9,5GB. Snapshot reserve can be increased and decreased on the fly.

```
cl1::> vol show -fields percent-snapshot-space -vserver v_example -volume
exvol
vserver    volume percent-snapshot-space
--------- ------ ----------------------
v_example exvol  0%


cl1::> vol modify -vserver v_example -volume exvol -percent-snapshot-space 0
```

7.3.4 Deleting snapshots.

To delete snapshots manually you can use the **snap delete** command.

```
cl1::*>   snap   delete   -vserver   v_example   -volume   exvol   -snapshot
example_.2017-08-20_0855

Warning: Deleting a Snapshot copy permanently removes any data that is
stored only in that
        Snapshot copy. Are you sure you want to delete Snapshot copy
        "example_.2017-08-20_0855" for volume "exvol" in Vserver
"v_example" ?
        {y|n}: y
```

7.3.4 FlexClones.

A FlexClone volume is a volume that is based on a snapshot in its parent volume. Since snapshots are read-only, it is problematic to test disaster recovery or any other form of data management for testing purposes. Instead of copying all the data of a volume to new volume, a FlexClone can be created that does not copy any data but uses the snapshot of another volume as a starting point. The FlexClone volume is a fully functional, and writeable volume in the same aggregate. FlexClones can be resized, independent of the size of the parent volume.

If you – after creation of the clone – decide that you want to have a real and independent copy of the parentvolume's data, you can split the clone so that all blocks are copied to the clone.

The creation of a FlexClone automatically generates a snapshot on the parent volume or an existing snapshot can be selected.

If a client accesses the clone volume, the client will see all files that are held in the snapshot of the parent. If the client modifies the contents of a file, the new blocks will need space in the clone volume. Also, if a client creates a new file in the clone, it will allocate blocks in the volumespace of the clone. Changes to the parent volume will not reflect in the clone, and vice versa.

```
Create a volume
cl1::> vol create -vserver v_nfs -volume pvol -aggregate n1_aggr1 -size
100m -junction-path /pvol

Clone the volume
cl1::> vol clone create -vserver v_nfs -flexclone cvol -parent-volume pvol

Split the clone
cl1::> vol clone split start -vserver v_nfs -flexclone cvol
```

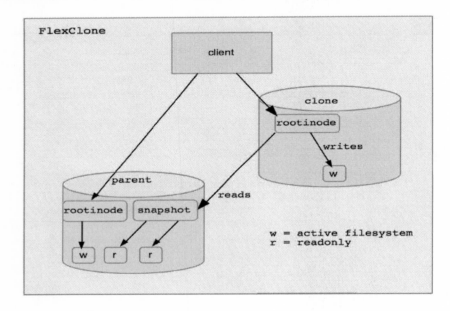

Use cases for FlexClones run from application testing to system deployment. It is a fast way of paralleling access to existing data with the ability to write new blocks.

7.4 Quality of Service.

To throttle the load on client and system operations to deliver predictable and consistent performance, you can create policy-groups to define a maximum throughput[1]. This allows for better performance of some objects versus other objects.

Qos can be defined for the following objects:

SVM with volumes
Volumes
LUNS
Files (think of VMs)

Controlling the maximum bandwidth is done by the use of *policy-groups*. A policy-group will be set with a maximum number of IOPS. Objects can then be connected to that policy-group, which will limit their bandwidth as configured.

In this simple example, three volumes are mounted to the same NFS-client. Two of these volumes will have a maximum throughput of 500iops, the third volume will get a maximum of 50iops. These values are ridiculously low, but because of the virtualized environment these examples are set in, this will give better results. The SVM has address `192.168.4.212`.

The steps in this example.

1. Create three volumes in the testvserver.
2. Check the export-policy.
3. Mount the volumes from the NFS client.
4. Generate IO from the client.
5. Create two policy-groups.
6. Connect the volumes to the policy-groups.
7. Monitor the load.

```
1. Create the volumes.
cl1::*> vol create -vserver testvserver -volume v1 -aggregate n2_aggr1 -size
500m -junction-path /v1
cl1::*> vol create -vserver testvserver -volume v2 -aggregate n2_aggr1 -size
500m -junction-path /v2
cl1::*> vol create -vserver testvserver -volume v3 -aggregate n2_aggr1 -size
500m -junction-path /v3

2. Check the export-policy.
cl1::*> export-policy rule show -vserver testvserver -policyname default
            Policy          Rule    Access   Client          RO
Vserver     Name            Index   Protocol Match           Rule
----------- --------------- ------- -------- --------------- ----
testvserver default         1       any      0.0.0.0/0       any
```

---

1   From ONTAP 9.2 up, Minimal throughput can also be defined.

3. In linux mount the rootvolume of the SVM.
```
root:/ # mkdir /mnt/212
root:/ # mount 192.168.4.212:/ /mnt/212
```

4. Generate some IO to all three volumes.
```
root:/ # cd /mnt/212
root:/mnt/212# while true ; do cp -r /etc/* v1; sleep 1; rm -rf v1/*; done&
root:/mnt/212# while true ; do cp -r /etc/* v2; sleep 1; rm -rf v2/*; done&
root:/mnt/212# while true ; do cp -r /etc/* v3; sleep 1; rm -rf v3/*; done&
```

5. Create two policy-groups
```
cl1::*> qos policy-group create -policy-group high -vserver testvserver
-max-throughput 500iops
cl1::*> qos policy-group create -policy-group low -vserver testvserver -max-
throughput 50iops
```

6. Connect the volumes to the policy-groups.
```
cl1::*> vol modify -vserver testvserver -volume v1 -qos-policy-group high
cl1::*> vol modify -vserver testvserver -volume v2 -qos-policy-group high
cl1::*> vol modify -vserver testvserver -volume v3 -qos-policy-group low
```

7. Monitor the load.
```
cl1::*> qos statistics performance show
Policy Group          IOPS     Throughput       Latency
-------------------   ------   --------------   ---------
-total-                587     313.01KB/s        3.78ms
high                   529     312.95KB/s        2.22ms
low                     53          0KB/s       19.78ms
_System-Work             5       0.06KB/s          0ms
-total-                395      22.43KB/s        4.40ms
high                   328      16.17KB/s        2.05ms
low                     53          0KB/s       20.04ms
_System-Work            14       6.26KB/s          0ms
```

7.5 Storage Efficiency.

To store your data efficiently you want to use little space for much data. So, lots of information, but with a small footprint. Using less hardware not only saves money on disks and controllers, but also on power and datacenter space.

In ONTAP, two major efficiency techniques are used: deduplication and compression.

7.5.1 Deduplication.

Deduplication is a technique to avoid writing duplicate blocks or to free already written duplicate blocks. Avoiding to write duplicate blocks is called *inline deduplication*. Freeing up duplicate blocks that have been written first, is called *post process deduplication*. Before ONTAP 9.2, deduplication was at the volume level. This meant that two different volumes were likely to hold the same blocks. From ONTAP 9.2, deduplication is at the aggregate level, which will obviously save a lot more diskspace.

7.5.2 Compression.

As with deduplication, compression is a technique to save diskspace. Compression – as the word says – compresses data. As with deduplication, compression can be done inline or post process.

There are two types of compression: adaptive and secondary. Adaptive compression means that there is a check for every 8KB of data whether it can be compressed for more than 50%. If that is the case, then the 8KB will be compressed. Compression of 8KB blocks gives a performance boost for random reads, because an 8KB block is uncompressed faster than a 32KB block, which is the size of the second compression-type: 32KB blocks. For sequential reads and write, secondary compression is advised. You can either configure adaptive compression or secondary compression.

7.5.3 Compaction.

Compaction is the technique of storing multiple smaller blocks in one 4KB block. After datablocks have been compressed these block can be candidates for being stored in a 4KB block, together with another block that is smaller than 4KB. Compaction – as do deduplication and compression – saves diskspace. Compaction is the last efficiency technique used, as part of the consistency point. It is a complement to inline adaptive compression.

Note: For inline deduplication and inline compaction you either need an ALL FLASH array, or a FLASH-Pool. In our examples we use the n2_aggr1 flash-pool.

Inline Compression and Compaction example, with post process deduplication.

In order to have some files with compressable data, 4KB, 8KB, and 32KB files were created. These files are also put in one tarfile. In total it amounts to some 150MB of ascii data. First we setup compression and compaction, and then we copy data into the volume. The SVM that we use is the 'testvserver' SVM. The volume we use is the 500MB volume 'v1' that is mounted to '/v1'. The lif that is used with the testvserver has IP 192.168.4.212.

The Linux client mounts the testvserver volume to /mnt/v1.

```
1. On Linux, create a mountpount, mount the volume and copy files to the
volume.
[root@lin70 ~]# mkdir /mnt/v1
[root@lin70 ~]# mount 192.168.4.212:/v1 /mnt/v1
[root@lin70 ~]# cp -r /mnt/eff/* /mnt/v1
```

2. To make sure we start from scratch, we turn off efficiency.
```
cl1::volume*> vol efficiency off -vserver testvserver -volume v1
cl1::volume*> vol efficiency undo -vserver testvserver -volume v1
```

3. We enable efficiency for the volume 'v1' for the SVM 'testvserver'.
```
cl1::volume*> vol efficiency on -vserver testvserver -volume v1
```

4. secondary compression is enabled and inline-compression is set to true.
```
cl1::volume*> vol efficiency modify -vserver testvserver -volume v1
-compression true -compression-type secondary  -inline-compression true
```

5. efficiency is started and compaction is set to true.
```
cl1::volume*> vol efficiency start -vserver testvserver -volume v1
-compaction true -scan-old-data true
```

6. copy some files to the volume
```
[root@lin70 ~]# cp -r /mnt/eff/* /mnt/v1/
```

7. After some time, ,list the space usage in the volume. In this case nearly half the space of 150MB is saved.
```
cl1::volume*> df -h -s -vserver testvserver -volume v1
/vol/v1/                      80MB         8192B            0%
```

8. Deduplicate the data stored in volume v1
```
cl1::*> vol efficiency start -vserver testvserver -volume v1 -dedupe true
-scan-old-data
```

9. List the space gained.
```
cl1::*> df -s -h -vserver testvserver -volume v1
Filesystem                    used         saved         %saved
/vol/v1/                      54MB         31MB          22%
```

An example script to generate some ascii content for compression purposes.

```
for letter in a b c d e f g h
do
 > 32k${letter}
done
for letter in a b c d e f g h
do
 for i in `seq 1 32768`
 do
        echo -n "${letter}" >> 32k${letter}
 done
done
```

Module 7 TRY THIS.

1. *Create a volume 'parentvol' in the SVM testvserver.*

2. *Export the volume with NFS and mount it from the linux client.*

3. *Create a file 'datafile' in the volume with content: original content.*

4. *Create a snapshot 'parentsnap' in the volume parentvol.*

5. *Change the content of the file to: new content.*

6. *Restore the file from the snapshot 'parentsnap'.*

7. *Create a flexible clone from using the snapshot 'parentsnap' as parent snapshot. Make sure the clone volume is mounted on '/cvol'.*

8. *Modify the content of 'datafile' in the clone volume to 'clone content'.*

9. *Delete the snapshot 'parentsnap' from the volume 'parentvol'.*
What happens?

10. *Split the cloned volume.*

8. NAS and SAN

The difference between NAS and SAN is basically one of the remote device access-level. In a NAS environment we speak of *File Level Access*. In a SAN environment we speak of *Block Level Access*. With Block Level Access, the client has the possibility and the responsibility to partition a disk and create a filesystem on the partition. In a NAS environment the client has no control over the filesystem or the device. In a NAS environment the client can retrieve files from and send files to a remote device by means of *file-handles*.

The NAS protocols supported in a NetApp environment are NFS and SMB. SMB is referred to CIFS. The SAN protocols supported by NetApp are FC, FCoE and iSCSI.

NAS or SAN	Protocol	Function
NAS	NFS	File level access for Linux/UNIX over TCP/IP
NAS	CIFS	File level access for windows/samba over TCP/IP
SAN	FCP	SCSI over Fibre Channel
SAN	FCoE	Fibre Channel over Ethernet
SAN	iSCSI	SCSI over TCP/IP

The different protocols can be combined at the SVM level, but not all protocols can be combined at the LIF level. NFS and CIFS can be combined, as can iSCSI and FCP. The data-protocol cannot be modified after the LIF is created. You will have to delete the LIF and recreate it, to change the data-protocol.

The data-protocols at the SVM level can be changed by using any of the following commands:

```
vserver modify -vserver <name> -allowed-protocols <protocol,...>
vserver add-protocol -vserver <name> -protocols <protocol,...>
vserver remove-protocol -vserver <name> -protocols <protocol,...>
```

From a network perspective it is important to realize that SAN LIFS do not failover and cannot be migrated to a different node or port, whereas NAS LIFS can failover based on the way the failover is configured.

8.1 NFS.

NFS (Network File System), is a client-server solution – originally developed by Sun Microsystems – that offers a distributed file system where the client accesses the server by mounting a remote volume or subdirectory to a local directory. To the client the files seem to be local. With NFS, files do not have to be moved between computers but can be centrally stored whilst being accessible by multiple clients simultaneously. The NFS server is configured at the SVM level. Volumes are assigned an *export-policy* that determines to which clients a volume is made accessible and with what permissions.

The export-policy holds *rules*. First an empty policy is created. Then rules are added to the policy.
To allow clients to mount a volume in the SVM namespace, the root volume of the SVM should also be accessible by the client. You can export the rootvolume read-only or read-write.

Clients accessing an exported resource will either mount the resource to a mount-point manually, via a file that contains the mounts that have to be done at boot-time (/etc/fstab), or via the automounter. When the client accesses the remote path on the server, the client has access by means of *file-handles*. The client has no control over the file system itself; (WAFL) in the case of ONTAP. This means that, if the NetApp administrator, resizes the volume that the client accesses, the available space the client sees, is automatically adjusted as well. This means great flexibility and resizing does not require any action on the client.

Another feature of NFS is that it a is stateless protocol. A client that loses access to the server, will retry to access the resource. So this means that, if there is a failover of a LIF, the client may regain access to the remote files after a retry. In the worst case – if something physical changes on the volume, like a snap restore – certain changes may result in a *'Stale NFS handle'* which means that the remote file system has to be remounted to the client's mount-point

In the example we use the following procedure:

1. Create an export-policy with rules for datavolumes and for the root volume.
2. Create a volume in SVM v_example.
3. Connect the export-policies to the volumes
4. Enable NFS for the SVM.
5. Create data LIF for the SVM.
6. Mount the volume from a Linux client.
7. Check client connection.

8.1.1 NFS example.

```
1. Create the policies and rules.

cl1::> export-policy create -vserver v_example -policyname datapol
cl1::*> export-policy rule create -vserver v_example -policyname datapol
-clientmatch 0.0.0.0/0 -rorule any -rwrule any -superuser any

cl1::*> export-policy create -vserver v_example -policyname rootpol
cl1::*> export-policy rule create -vserver v_example -policyname rootpol
-clientmatch 0.0.0.0/0 -rorule any -rwrule none

2. Create a datavolume and mount it.

cl1::*> vol create -vserver v_example -volume datavol -aggregate n1_aggr1
-size 500m -junction-path /datavol -policy datapol

3. Connect the export-policies.

cl1::*> vol modify -vserver v_example -volume datavol -policy datapol
cl1::*> vol modify -vserver v_example -volume rv -policy rootpol

4. Enable NFS.

cl1::> nfs on -vserver v_example

5. Create a LIF.

cl1::> net int create -vserver v_example  -lif nfs223 -role data -data-
protocol nfs -home-node cl1-01 -home-port e0d -address 192.168.4.223
-netmask 255.255.255.0

6. Access the volume from the Linux client.

root:/ # mkdir /mnt/223
root:/ # mount 192.168.4.223:/datavol /mnt/223

7. Check the network connections to the SVM.

cl1::*> network connections active show-clients -vserver v_example
Node            Vserver Name    Client IP Address  Count
--------------  --------------  -----------------  ------
cl1-01
                v_example       192.168.4.158              1

Check client access to all volumes in the SVM.

cl1::> export-policy check-access -vserver v_example -volume datavol
-client-ip 192.168.4.223 -authentication-method sys -protocol nfs3 -access-
type read
                                     Policy     Policy        Rule

Path      Policy     Owner     Owner Type  Index Access
-------   ---------- --------- ----------  ----- ----------
/         rootpol    rv        volume        1 read
/datavol  datapol    nfsvol    volume        1 read
```

The authentication method for rorule and rwrule can be any of *any none never krb5 krb5i krb5p ntlm sys*
The *-superuser* argument allows the rootuser of the client to actually be treated as user id 0. This is common practice for example in the case of Vmware whereby Virtual Machine files are written by uid 0.

The *-allow-suid* setting honor the SUID bit or not. If the SUID bit is honored, the programme that is executed, will be executed with the user id of the owner, which is a security risk. By default it is switched to on.
The -allow-dev setting allow for the creation of devices or not.

To show all exported volumes to clients the *-showmount* option should be enabled.

```
cl1::*> vserver nfs modify -vserver v_example -showmount enabled
```

To export a volume from the vserver v_example, the volume will have to be created, mounted and should have an export-policy that actually exports. It is important that the root volume of the SVM is also exported. The client is not able to access the namespace otherwise.

On the NFS client, a directory functions as the mount-point for the remote volume. The client can use the mount command to setup a session between client and server.

```
root:~# showmount -e 192.168.4.223
Export list for 192.168.4.223:
/exvol (everyone)
/      (everyone)

root:~# mkdir /mnt/223
root:~# mount 192.168.4.223:/exvol /mnt/223
```

8.2 NFS version.

ONTAP 9+ supports the following nfs versions and features[1]:

NFS v3	NFS 4.0
NFS v4.1	NFS 4.0 Referral Support
NFS v4.1 Parallel NFS	NFS 4.0 read and write delegation

---

1   This is not a complete list of features.

8.2.1 NFS v3.

Version 3 is commonly used in Linux and UNIX based environment and VMware environments, and is enabled by default. It supports caching (-cto) and dynamic retries. Version 3 is not famous for its security. If security is an issue, version 4.x is a better option.

Still NFS v3 is still a widely used protocol-version.

Enabling NFS for an SVM will automatically only enable NFSv3.

```
cl1::*> nfs on -vserver testvserver

cl1::*> nfs show -vserver testvserver

                                  Vserver: testvserver
                       General NFS Access: true
        RPC GSS Context Cache High Water Mark: 0
                    RPC GSS Context Idle: 0
                                  NFS v3: enabled
                                NFS v4.0: disabled
```

8.2.2 Version 4.0 Referrals.

If the client accesses a LIF that is hosted by a cluster-node that does not host the volume, ONTAP will make the client mount via a LIF that is actually hosted by the cluster-node that holds the volume. To enable NFS v4.0-referrals, you should also enable v4-fsid-change, and v4.0.
 If clients do not support NFSv4.0 referrals, set v4.0-referrals to disabled.

In the example we follow this procedure:

1.	Create two LIFS, one on node1 192.168.4.224 and one on node2 192.168.4.225.
2.	Create a volume that is hosted by the data aggregate on node2.
3.	Create the export-policies – for the root volume and data volume.
4.	Connect the policies to the necessary volumes.
5.	Enable NFS for the SVM.
6.	Enable v4-fsid-change, v4.0-referrals and v4.0 for the nfs SVM.
7.	On Linux, mount the data volume, using the address not local to the volume
8.	On Linux, use netstat to check what ip address was used.

Note: In the NFS 4.0 referral example, we go over the creation of a volume, export-policies and LIFS again. We dealt with that in the example in paragraph 8.1.1, but we want to make sure that you can do test the examples in random order.

1. *Create two LIFS, on node1 and on node2.*

```
cl1::*> net int create -vserver v_example -lif n1_lif -role data -data-
protocol nfs -home-node cl1-01 -home-port e0d -address 192.168.4.224
-netmask 255.255.255.0

cl1::*> net int create -vserver v_example -lif n2_lif -role data -data-
protocol nfs -home-node cl1-02 -home-port e0d -address 192.168.4.225
-netmask 255.255.255.0
```

2. Create a volume in the node2 aggregate.

```
cl1::*> vol create -vserver v_example -volume n2_vol -aggregate n2_aggr1
-size 100m -junction-path /n2_vol -policy datapol
```

3. Create the export policies for the data volumes and root volume.

```
cl1::*> export-policy create -vserver v_example -policyname datapol
cl1::*> export-policy rule create -vserver v_example -policyname datapol
-clientmatch 0.0.0.0/0 -rorule any -rwrule any -superuser any

cl1::*> export-policy create -vserver v_example -policyname rootpol
cl1::*> export-policy rule create -vserver v_example -policyname rootpol
-clientmatch 0.0.0.0/0 -rorule any -rwrule none
```

4. connect the policies with the volumes.

```
cl1::*> vol modify -vserver v_example -volume n2_vol -policy datapol
cl1::*> vol modify -vserver v_example -volume rv -policy rootpol
```

5. enable nfs for the SVM.

```
cl1::> nfs on -vserver v_example
```

6. Enable v4-fsid-change, v4.0-referrals and v4.0.

```
cl1::*> vserver nfs modify -vserver v_example -v4-fsid-change enabled
cl1::*> vserver nfs modify -vserver v_example -v4.0-referrals enabled
cl1::*> vserver nfs modify -vserver v_example -v4.0 enabled
```

7. Access the volume from your Linux client and use the LIF that is hosted on node1.

```
root:/ # mkdir /mnt/224
root:/ # mount 192.168.4.224:/n2_vol /mnt/224
```

8. with netstat check that the client uses the address (225) local to volume.

```
root:/ # netstat -an |grep -i established|grep 225
tcp        0        0 192.168.4.158:842   192.168.4.225:2049   ESTABLISHED
```

8.2.3 NFS v4.1 Parallel NFS

Parallel NFS (pNFS) gives clients access to the files distributed across two or more servers in parallel. Parallel NFS will be beneficial for performance since it allows NFS clients to perform read/write operations directly and in parallel, bypassing the NFS server as a potential bottleneck. Parallel NFS in ONTAP is enabled by default if NFS v4.1 is enabled. Disabling Parallel NFS is done by disabling the *v4.1-pnfs* option.

How does pNFS work?

It is a two stage process. The pNFS enabled client mounts a volume in the cluster, by connecting to a LIF somewhere in the cluster. the node that services the mount, becomes the metadataserver, but not necessarily the dataserver. If the volume is hosted by the node that service the mount, that node is also the dataserver.
   The data request that comes from the client – either read or write – will result in a VLDB check to determine the location of the volume that is requested. If the node is determined, then the Vifmgr is used to determine the LIF that is on the node that also hosts the volume. The client will then access the node that holds the LIF and volume directly, no remount needed.
   So, there is always a metadataserver and a dataserver, and they don't necessarily have to be the same physical node.

Note: pNFS and v4.0-referrals cannot be enabled both. They are mutually exclusive.

To successfully enable pNFS, NFSv4.0, NFSv4.1 also have to be enabled. For NFSv4.0 the identity-mapping-domain has to be specified. This includes additional settings outside the ONTAP settings.

8.2.4 Enabling pNFS.

```
1. Enable pNFS.

cl1::*> vserver nfs modify -vserver v_example -v4.0 enabled -v4.1 enabled
-v4.1-pnfs enabled -v4-id-domain netapp.com

2. From the Linux client, mount the volume.

root:/ # mount -o v4.1 192.168.4.224:/n2_vol /mnt/224
```

Note: *id-domain* settings require configurations that are external from ONTAP and are beyond the scope of this book.

8.3 CIFS.

ONTAP 9 supports SMB version 1, 2 and 3. When referring to SMB we still use the term CIFS. So we talk of the cifs protocol and of a cifs SVM. Cifs allows users to access shared data from ONTAP volumes or qtrees[1], as does NFS.

To allow access to a volume for Windows clients, the SVM has to either be part of a workgroup, or it has to be a computer in an Active Directory domain. So, you can have multiple cifs SVMs, each of which is part of a different Active Directory domain. The cifs SVM functions as an Active Directory Member server to authenticate users that access data.

Another functionality of an SVM that is configured with cifs, is that it can function as a domain tunnel. So the SVM not necessarily services data, but authenticates users or groups that access the cluster for administration purposes. This way Active Directory users can use the same account information to login to the cluster.

For the cifs SVM to function properly it is of importance that the time-skew is no bigger than five minutes with respect to the Active Directory environment. If the time difference is more than five minutes, your cifs environment will not function. Also, dns should be setup for the SVM before you can add

We will see an example of both cifs purposes.

To configure the SVM as a cifs server these should be the steps.

8.3.1 Setting up a cifs SVM.

To set up a cifs SVM, this is a possible workflow.

1. Add the SVM as a computer to Active Directory.
2. Create a data volume.
3. Create a share for the volume.
4. Set the access for the share. (optional)

In the example below, in order to be able to create a computer in Active Directory, you will have supply the authorized user and password. If this is a problem, you can also have the computer created by the Active Directory administrator, and a user has to be created in Active Directory that is able to manage the Computer that was created for you.

The volume that you create should be mounted – via a junction-path – otherwise it will not be accessible, even though it is shared.

To share the volume you must specify the *pathname* and the *sharename* via which the client can access the volume.

---

1   A qtree is a directory with two special features: security-style and quotas.

8.3.2 Create the computer in Active Directory.

```
cl1::> vserver create -vserver cifs_svm -subtype default -rootvolume rv
-aggregate n1_aggr1 -rootvolume-security-style ntfs

cl1::> net int create -vserver cifs_svm -lif cifs_228 -role data -data-
protocol cifs -home-node cl1-01 -home-port e0d -address 192.168.4.228
-netmask 255.255.255.0 -status-admin up


cl1::> dns create -vserver cifs_svm -domains netapp.local -name-servers
192.168.4.247


cl1::> vserver cifs create -vserver cifs_svm -cifs-server CIFS_SVM -domain
netapp.local -ou CN=Computers
In order to create an Active Directory machine account for the CIFS server,
you must supply the name and password of a
Windows account with sufficient privileges to add computers to the
"CN=Computers" container within the "NETAPP.LOCAL"
domain.

Enter the user name: administrator

Enter the password:



cl1::> cifs show
                Server    StatusDomain/Workgroup Authentication
Vserver         Name      Admin Name             Style
----------      -------   ----- ----------       ----------
cifs_svm        CIFS_SVM  up    NETAPP            domain
```

8.3.3 Create a data volume and a share.

```
cl1::> vol create -vserver cifs_svm -volume cifs_data -aggregate n2_aggr1
-size 500m -junction-path /cifs_data

Warning: The export-policy "default" has no rules in it. The volume will
therefore be inaccessible.
Do you want to continue? {y|n}: y
[Job 335] Job succeeded: Successful

cl1::> cifs share create -share-name cifsdata -path /cifs_data
```

8.3.4 Access the share from Windows.

To access the newly created share – in Windows – you map a network drive to the following Folder.

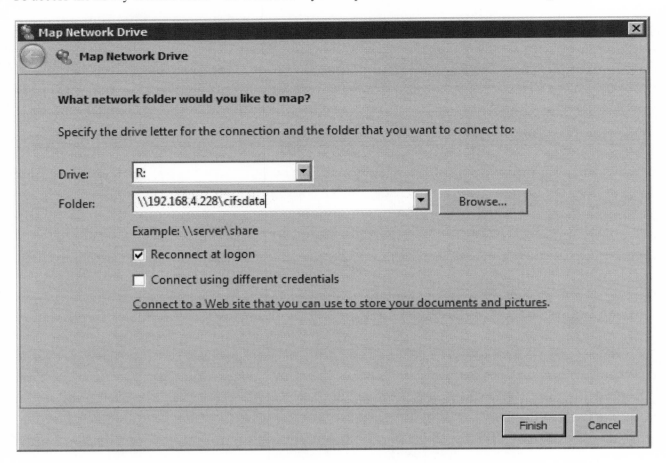

8.3.5 Share a qtree.

You can share a qtree the following way.

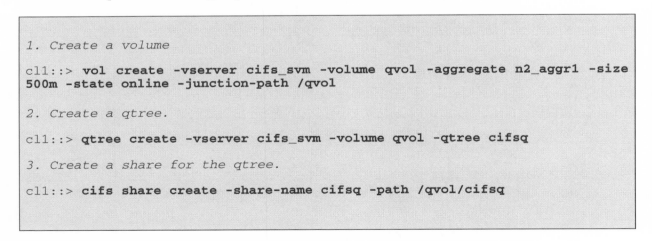

```
1. Create a volume

cl1::> vol create -vserver cifs_svm -volume qvol -aggregate n2_aggr1 -size
500m -state online -junction-path /qvol

2. Create a qtree.

cl1::> qtree create -vserver cifs_svm -volume qvol -qtree cifsq

3. Create a share for the qtree.

cl1::> cifs share create -share-name cifsq -path /qvol/cifsq
```

8.3.6 Administrative shares.

After the creation of the cifs SVM, these three default (hidden) shares will be available.

ipc$	For Netapp use (named pipes). Cannot be renamed or deleted.
admin$	For remote administration of the SVM. Cannot be renamed or deleted.
c$	SVM root volume. ACL - Administrator / Full Control.

8.3.7 Share access.

You can change the access to the share.

```
c11::> cifs share access-control modify -vserver cifs_svm -share cifsdata
-user-or-group everyone -permission read
```

8.3.8 Delete the cifs svm.

To delete the cifs svm, you will also delete it from Active Directory. If you still have active shares, you will get a warning.

```
c11::> cifs delete -vserver cifs_svm

In order to delete an Active Directory machine account for the CIFS server,
you must supply the name and password of a Windows account with sufficient
privileges to remove computers from the "NETAPP.LOCAL" domain.

Enter the user name: administrator



Enter the password: ********

Warning: There are one or more shares associated with this CIFS server
         Do you really want to delete this CIFS server and all its shares?
{y|n}: y
```

8.4 Security-styles.

Since ONTAP uses WAFL – which is a UNIX filesystem – every file has an inode. The inode contains the file-permissions. The permissions are UNIX permissions. Basic UNIX permissions are *rwx*. This triplet is created for every file and contains an entry for the userid (uid), groupid (gid) and for the rest of the world(others).

Symbol	meaning
r	Read the contents of a file or list the contents of a directory.
w	Write the contents of a file or modify the contents of a directory.
x	Execute the file if it is a program or a script, and make the directory to your current working directory.
–	No permission.

In the following example, the owner has *read/write* access, the group and others have *read* access.

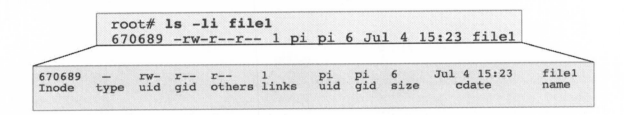

Because WAFL also supports windows clients to create files, the UNIX inode with its UNIX permissions does not suffice. Windows based files use Access Control Lists (ACLs). This is why a WAFL inode has an additional pointer to an xinode, which contains the ACL for windows users' authorization.

An Access Control List (ACL) has zero or more Access Control Entries (ACEs). An ACE contains a *principal*. Usually this is either a user or a group. It could be a user, group, or computer in an Active Directory database on a domain controller, or a local user. There are "virtual" groups such as "Everyone" and "Authenticated Users."

The security-style determines what is used (inode or ACL) to determine the permissions of the file. There are three security-styles available in ONTAP.

Security-style	Result
Unix	Only the inode is used for permissions.
NTFS	Only the xinode is used for permissions.
Mixed	The last changed is (inode or xinode) is active.

8.4.1 Volumes and qtrees.

A security-style can be set on a volume or on a qtree. Some examples.

```
cl1::> vol modify -vserver nas_svm -volume nas_volume -security-style unix

cl1::> qtree modify -vserver nas_svm -volume nas_volume -qtree "cifs_tree"
-security-style ntfs

cl1::> qtree cl1::> qtree modify -vserver nas_svm -volume nas_volume -qtree
"nas_tree" -security-style mixed
```

In the above example, the UNIX inode is used to determine permissions in the volume "nas_volume". This means that, by default, Windows clients will not be able to access this volume to create or modify files. The qtree "cifs_tree" will only support Windows clients to access and manage files. The qtree "nas_tree" supports windows as well as UNIX access.

Mixed security-style is generally not recommended. Changes by Windows users can affect functionality for UNIX users and the other way around. A use-case for mixed security-style would be that one side – e.g. Windows – writes files where the other side – UNIX – only needs read access. But even then...

8.4.2 User mapping.

To allow a Windows client to manage files in a unix-security-style environment, Windows users can be mapped to UNIX users. And UNIX users can be mapped to Windows users to access ntfs-security-style environments.

Examples of mapping users.

Accounts in the Windows administrators group are mapped to root, by default. So if a Windows administrator accesses a share, the administrator is allowed to create and delete files, even though the security-style of the share is UNIX. The first example will undo that mapping.

```
cl1::*> vol show -vserver nas_svm -volume nas_volume -fields security-style
vserver volume      security-style
------- ---------- --------------
nas_svm nas_volume unix

cl1::*> vserver cifs options modify -vserver nas_svm -is-admin-users-
mapped-to-root-enabled false
```

This will result in the administrators group from AD not being able to write the share if the security-style is unix.

The UNIX user *thompson_k* is mapped to the Windows user *bill* in the *ENG* domain.

```
cl1::*> vserver name-mapping create -vserver nas_svm  -direction unix-win
-position 1 -pattern thompson_k -replacement "ENG\\bill"
```

As seen in the example, you need the following to setup mapping:

vserver	The name of the SVM **(nas_svm)**
direction	krb-unix|win-unix|unix-win **(unix-win)**
position	Sequential entry in the SVM **(1)**
pattern text	Source entity **(thompson_k)**
replacement text	Target entity **(ENG\\bill)**
Ip/subnet | hostname	The clients ip/subnet or hostname **(optional)**

The following example shows that there is a mapping from the *windows* account *finance\\henry* from ip *192.168.4.10* to the *UNIX backup* user.

```
cl1::> vserver name-mapping show -vserver nas_svm -position 3
Vserver:    nas_svm
Direction: win-unix
Position Hostname          IP Address/Mask
-------- ---------------- ----------------
3        -                 192.168.4.10/24    Pattern: finance\\henry
                                              Replacement: backup
```

8.5 iSCSI.

With iSCSI, a logical device (LUN) is mapped to a client machine. This client machine will – when scanning its SCSI bus – detect a new disk-device. The superuser or administrator of the client has to configure the disk in a way appropriate for the client OS and can create a file system on the disk-device. The configuration and management of the disk-device is not under control of ONTAP. This has implications for managing the the device for both ends. ONTAP is not aware of the contents of the blocks written by the client OS and the client OS may be misinformed about the actual block allocations by ONTAP.
There are ways to match the two views by using tools like *Snapdrive*, or *unmap* commands run on clients.

Note: Since we aim to exemplify the ONTAP cli, we will not discuss the workings of all of these tools.

In a SAN environment, the client that wants the logical device is called an *initiator*, the SVM offering the device is called the *target*. In ONTAP, the SVM that functions as a target will have a target alias created for the client to connect to. You can have multiple SVMs running as an iSCSI target. And, of course, a single SVM can hold multiple luns.

8.5.1 igroup, luns and iqns.

A lun is a file in WAFL. This lun can reside in a volume or in a qtree. For the client to be able to access the lun, the client must be logged in to the target (1). The target has an igroup that holds the initiator's iqn (2). The lun is mapped to the igroup(3). The client gets access to the lun (4).

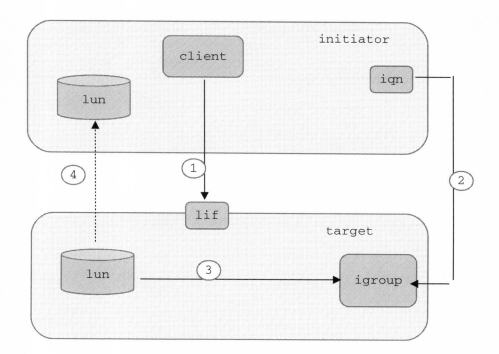

8.5.2 Create an iSCSI SVM.

Steps to create an iSCSI SVM:

1. Create the SVM.
2. Create the iSCSI target in the SVM.
3. Create an iSCSI LIF.
4. Create an igroup.
5. Populate the igroup.
6. Create a volume.
7. Create a lun.
8. Map the lun.

```
1 Create the SVM.
cl1::*> vserver create -vserver v_iscsi -subtype default -rootvolume rv
-aggregate n1_aggr1 -rootvolume-security-style unix

2. Create iSCSI target.
cl1::*> iscsi create -vserver v_iscsi


3. Create a LIF.
cl1::*> net int create -vserver v_iscsi -lif iscsi_211 -role data -data-
protocol iscsi -home-node cl1-01 -home-port e0d -address 192.168.4.211
-netmask 255.255.255.0

4. Create an igroup.
cl1::> igroup create -vserver v_iscsi -igroup wingroup -protocol mixed
-ostype windows

5. Populate the igroup.
cl1::> igroup add -vserver v_iscsi -igroup wingroup -initiator iqn.1991-
05.com.microsoft:win-dhn5u460s93

6. Create a volume.
cl1::> vol create -vserver v_iscsi -volume lunvol -aggregate n1_aggr1 -size
1g

7. Create a lun.
cl1::> lun create -vserver v_iscsi -path /vol/lunvol/winlun -size 800m
-ostype windows

8. Map the lun.
cl1::> lun map -vserver v_iscsi -path /vol/lunvol/winlun -igroup wingroup
```

8.5.3 Client login.

We will demonstrate a windows client login in as well as a Linux client login in to get access to the iSCSI lun,

For Windows.
1. Open iSCSI initiator and click Discovery.

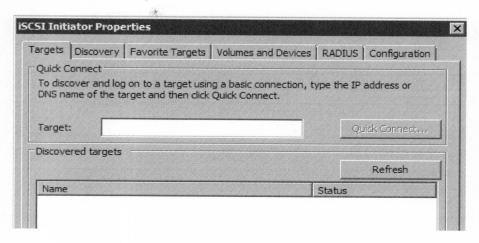

2. Click Discover Portal.

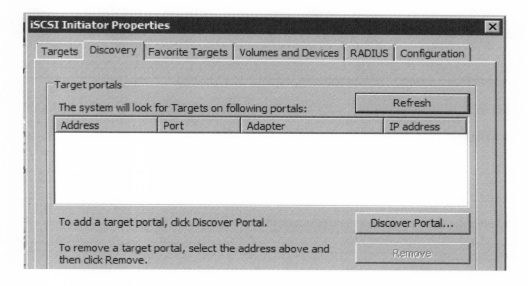

3. Enter the ip address of the target SVM and click OK.

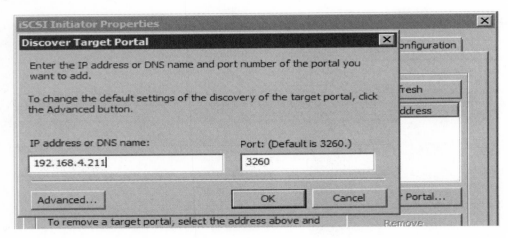

4. The target is inactive. Select the target and click Connect.

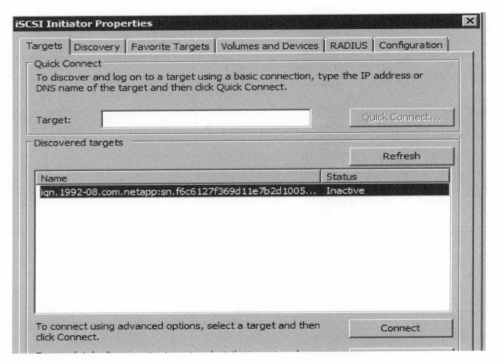

5. Click OK.

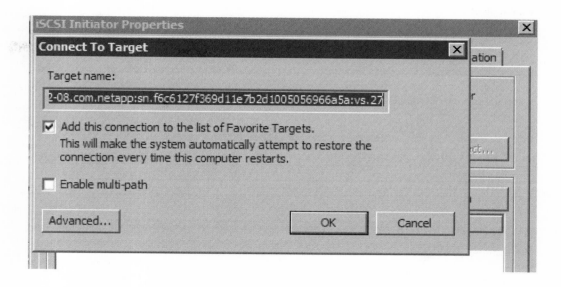

6. The target should be connected.

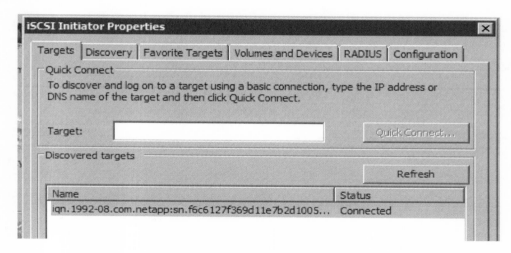

7. Depending on the OS version, you should rescan the disks in Disk Management and the new disk should be available for setting up.

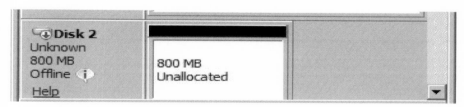

Linux and iSCSI.

---

1. Install iscsi initiator utils and query your initiator id.

```
[root@lin70 ~]# yum -y install iscsi-initiator-utils
[root@lin70 ~]# cat /etc/iscsi/initiatorname.iscsi
InitiatorName=iqn.1994-05.com.redhat:42421ad0974e
```

2. Create a linux igroup and add the initiator.

```
cl1::> igroup create -vserver v_iscsi -igroup lingroup -protocol mixed
linux
cl1::> igroup add -vserver v_iscsi -igroup lingroup -initiator iqn.1994-
05.com.redhat:42421ad0974e
```

3. Create and map the lun.

```
cl1::> lun create -vserver v_iscsi  -path /vol/lunvol/linuxlun -size 800m
-ostype linux
cl1::> lun map -vserver v_iscsi -path /vol/lunvol/linuxlun -igroup lingroup
```

4. Login to the target.

```
[root@lin70 ~]# iscsiadm -m discovery -t sendtargets -p 192.168.4.211
[root@lin70 /]# service iscsi restart
```

5. Check the availability of the new disk.
```
[root@lin70 /]# fdisk -l |grep sd

Disk /dev/sdd: 838 MB, 838860800 bytes, 1638400 sectors
(output skipped)
```

Now you can partition the new disk and create a file system.

8.6 Fractional Reserve.

The 'problem' with luns is that the administration of the WAFL file system is not a one-on-one with the administration of the file system that the client creates on the lun. If a snapshot is created on a volume that holds a LUN, then blocks that belong to the lun will also be snapshotted.

If the administrator of the client removes files from its file system, then the blocks belonging to the removed – or modified – file will not be freed in WAFL, because they are held by the snapshot. This means that the client view of the file system differs from the actual situation in WAFL.

For example:
1. the client created a 1GB file system on a 1GB lun that was created in a 1GB volume.
2. The client fills the file system with 80% of data.
3. A snapshot is created in the volume.
4. The client removes half of the files in the file system.

The result will be that the administration of the client's file system says that there if 60% of space available in the file system, whereas the snapshot in WAFL still holds the 80% of blocks. If the client starts writing files again, the lun will be full after adding 200MB, instead of the expected 600MB.

To prevent this, Fractional Reserve is enabled by default. Fractional Reserve means that – if a snapshot is present – every block that is written in the lun, will additionally be reserved in the volume. This means that in the previous example, the lun should not be larger than half the volume size. Now, even if the lun is 95% full, the 95% of reserved blocks in the volume will support a complete lun overwrite.

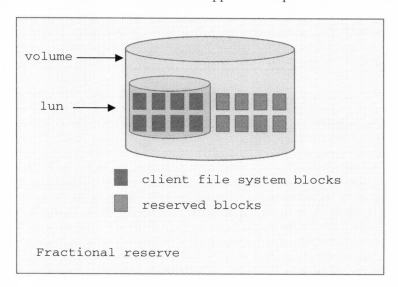

8.6.1 Fractional Reserve at work.

In paragraph 8.5.3 a Linux iscsi lun was created and accessed by linux. In the next example this lun is partitioned, a filesystem is added and mounted. A snapshot is created in the volume and fractional reserve is enabled. Then we create some files and check whether additional blocks are reserved in the volume.

The steps:

1. create a partition in the disk.
2. create a filesystem in the partition and mount it.
3. create a snapshot in the volume and enable fractional reserve.
4. create a file in the lun.
5. list the reserved blocks in the volume.

```
1. partition the disk sdd.

[root@lin70 ~]# fdisk /dev/sdd
(output skipped)

Command (m for help): n
Partition type:
   p   primary (0 primary, 0 extended, 4 free)
   e   extended
Select (default p):
Using default response p
Partition number (1-4, default 1):
First sector (2048-1023999, default 2048):
Using default value 2048
Last sector, +sectors or +size{K,M,G} (2048-1023999, default 1023999):
Using default value 1023999
Partition 1 of type Linux and of size 499 MiB is set

Command (m for help): w
(output skipped)

Syncing disks.

2. create a filesystem, a mountpoint and mount it.

[root@lin70 ~]# mkfs /dev/sdd1; mkdir /lun; mount /dev/sdd1 /lun

3. create a snapshot in the volume and enable fractional reserve.

cl1::> snapshot create -vserver v_iscsi -volume lunvol -snapshot snap1
cl1::> vol modify -volume lunvol -fractional-reserve 100%

4. create a file.

[root@lin70 ~]# cd /lun ; dd if=/dev/zero of=file bs=1024 count=50240

5. list the snapshot reserve.

cl1::> df -h -r lunvol -vserver v_iscsi
Filesystem                total      used      avail    reserved  Mounted on
/vol/lunvol/              1024MB     568MB     455MB       66MB    ---
```

In the example you see that allocating blocks in the lun results in reserving blocks for lun overwrite in the remaining space of the volume.

Module 8 TRY THIS.

1. Create a volume 'nfs1' in the SVM 'testvserver' that supports the nfs
   protocol with junction-path /nfsvol

2. Create an export-policy 'datapol' that allows the Linux vm to mount the
exported volume with read and write access
    and treat uid 0 as uid 0.

3. From Linux, mount the volume to the mountpoint /mnt/nfsvol
    (the testvserver has address 192.168.4.212.)

4. Create some files in the volume.

5. Create a volume 'cifs1' in the SVM 'testvserver' that supports the nfs
   protocol with junction-path /cifsvol

6. Create a dns server and a cifs server for the SVM testvserver.
    (use your own domain-name and server IP.)

7. Create a cifs share for the volume 'cifs1'.

8. From the windows command-tool map a driveletter to the share.

9. Snapmirror.

Snapmirror is NetApp's native replication service that allows you to create relationships of different types. Relationships can exist between different volumes or different SVMs. The available snapmirror types are listed below.

A-synchronous snapmirror was the only snapmirror form supported until ONTAP 9.5 arrived. ONTAP 9.5 and later support Synchronous Snapmirror. Destination volumes are always of the type DP when created. You cannot change the type afterwards.

Type	Function
DP	For disaster recovery (DataProtection)
XDP	For disk to disk backup (ExtendedDataProtection)
LS	LoadShare, primarily for SVM rootvol protection
RST	Restore, automatically created during a restore
TDP	Transition Data Protection for migration from 7-mode to Clustered ONTAP.

9.1 SVMs and Clusters.

Snapmirror relationships can be created in the following fashions:

relationship	type
Two volumes in the same SVM	DP, XDP, LS
Two volumes in two different SVMs in the same cluster	DP, XDP
Two volumes in two different SVMs in two different clusters	DP, XDP, TDP
Two different SVMs in two different clusters (SVMDR)	DP

As discussed in module 6, to setup inter-SVM and inter-cluster needs peering of the different entities before snapmirror can be setup. This is a fixed order:

1.	peering of clusters
2.	peering of svms
3.	create snapmirror
4.	remove snapmirror
5.	unpeer svms
6.	unpeer clusters

9.2 Loadshare Snapmirror.

A loadshare snapmirror currently is only used to snapmirror the rootvolume of an SVM. Netapp recommends to snapmirror the root volume of an SVM to every node in the cluster.

To setup a loadshare relation for the root volume of the SVM, create a destination volume of the type DP on every node in the cluster. The initialization is performed with the initialize-ls-set argument. The update is performed with the update-ls-set argument. NetApp recommends to update every hour.
Creation of a new volume results in the junction-path to be available for clients only after the update has run. When clients mount a volume, they always have to access the rootvolume first. If the rootvolume is mounted, it is mounted readonly by default. If the volume is mounted read-only, then always the snapmirror destination volume is used, and not the source volume. So the junction-paths in the root volume are only present on the destination volume after the update. It may be an idea to run the **snapmirror update-ls-set** command at the end of the volume creation procedure.

```
cl1::*> vol create -vserver v_example -volume rv_dest_1 -aggregate n2_aggr1
-size 1g -type DP
cl1::*> snapmirror create -source-path v_example:rv -destination-path
v_example:rv_dest_1 -type LS
cl1::*> snapmirror initialize-ls-set -source-path v_example:rv
cl1::*> snapmirror update-ls-set -source-path v_example:rv
```

9.2.1 Promote a destination.

If you lose the original root volume of an SVM, you can promote a destination volume. This volume will then become the active root volume. If you have multiple destinations, the volume that you promote, will automatically take over the relationships.
  In the next example, we have a root volume with to destinations in a LoadShare relation. Then we promote one of the two destinations. The promotion will try to remove the original volume if still present. First, show the relations.

```
cl1::*> snapmirror show

                                                                    Progress
Source              Destination Mirror  Relationship   Total                Last
Path          Type  Path        State   Status         Progress  Healthy
Updated
-----------   ----  ----------- ------- -------------- --------- -------
---------
cl1://v_example/rv
              LS    cl1://v_example/rv_dest_1
                                Snapmirrored
                                        Idle           -         true      -
                    cl1://v_example/rv_dest_2
                                Snapmirrored
                                        Idle           -         true      -
```

Then promote one of the destination volumes.

```
cl1::*> snapmirror promote -destination-path v_example:rv_dest_1
cl1::*> snapmirror show

Progress
Source                  Destination Mirror  Relationship   Total               Last
Path            Type    Path        State   Status         Progress  Healthy   Updated
----------      ----    ----------- ------- -------------- --------- -------    --------
cl1://v_example/rv_dest_1
                LS      cl1://v_example/rv_dest_2
                                    Snapmirrored
                                            Idle           -         true      -
```

9.3 Snapmirror DR.

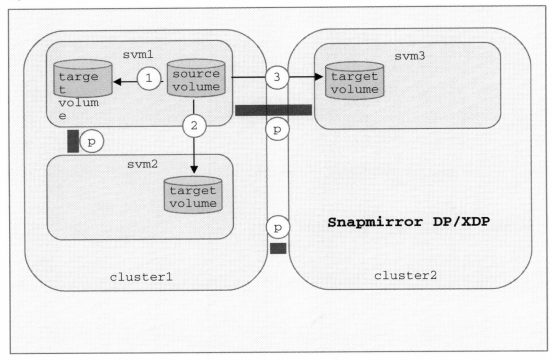

In a snapmirror DR relation, the source volume is writable, the destination volume is read-only at all times, until the relationship is broken. Snapmirror DR relationships are typically used between two different clusters in two different datacenters. The distance between the two datacenters is unlimited. The destination volume can be accessed by clients for reading.

The snapmirror relationship will get a snapmirror policy and a schedule.

In the next example we do a complete runthrough of setting up a snapmirror relation, perform a disaster recovery test and reestablish the original situation.

```
1. Check cluster peering.
2. Create two SVMs, one on the first cluster and one on the second.
3. Peer the two SVMs.
4. Create a source and destination volume.
5. Setup and initialize the snapmirror.
6. Create a snapmirror policy and schedule it.
```

9.3.1 Snapmirror DR example.

```
1. Are the two clusters peered?

cl1::> cluster peer show
cl2      1-80-000008      Available     ok
cl2::> cluster peer show
cl1      1-80-000008      Available      ok

2. Create two SVMs, one on every cluster.

cl1::> vserver create v_src -subtype default -rootvolume rv -aggregate
n1_aggr1 -rootvolume-security-style unix
cl2::>  vserver create -vserver v_dst -subtype default -rootvolume rv
-aggregate aggr1 -rootvolume-security-style unix

3. Peer the two SVMs.

cl1::> vserver peer create -vserver v_src -peer-vserver v_dst -applications
snapmirror -peer-cluster cl2
cl2::> vserver peer accept -vserver v_dst -peer-vserver v_src

4. Create a source and a destination volume. The destination volume should
be of the type DP!

cl1::> vol create -vserver v_src -volume src_dp -aggregate n1_aggr1 -size
500m -junction-path /src_dp
cl2::>  vol create -vserver v_dst -volume dst_dp -aggregate aggr1 -size
500m -type dp

5. Setup snapmirror and initialize.

cl2::> snapmirror create -source-path v_src:src_dp -destination-path
v_dst:dst_dp
cl2::> snapmirror initialize -destination-path v_dst:dst_dp

6. Create a policy for the snapmirror and schedule it.

cl2::> snapmirror policy create -vserver v_dst -policy dp_pol -type async-
mirror
cl2::> snapmirror modify -destination-path v_dst:dst_dp -schedule 5min
-policy dp_pol
```

To actually perform a DR. We will need some data on the source that gets replicated to the destination. We setup an NFS share, access in from the Linux client, put some files in the volume and run a snapmirror update. Once the files are replicated. We break the relation and start working on the destination.

9.3.2 NFS data to snapmirror source.

```
1. Setup a data lif for both SVMs and create export policies with rules.

c11::> net int create -vserver v_src -lif nas_210 -role data -data-protocol
nfs -home-node c11-01 -home-port e0d -address 192.168.4.210 -netmask
255.255.255.0
c12::> net int create -vserver v_dst -lif nas_212 -role data -data-protocol
nfs -home-node c12-01 -home-port e0c -address 192.168.4.212 -netmask
255.255.255.0

c11::> export-policy create -vserver v_src -policyname v_src_pol
c11::> export-policy rule create -vserver v_src -policyname v_src_pol
-clientmatch 0.0.0.0/0 -rorule any -rwrule any -superuser any

c12::> export-policy create -vserver v_dst -policyname v_dst_pol
c12::> export-policy rule create -vserver v_dst -policyname v_dst_pol
-clientmatch 0.0.0.0/0 -rorule any -rwrule any -superuser any

3. Connect the policies to the volumes, be sure not to forget the root
volume and enable nfs for both SVMs.

c11::> vol modify -vserver v_src -volume rv -policy v_src_pol
c11::> vol modify -vserver v_src -volume src_dp -policy v_src_pol
c12::> vol modify -vserver v_dst -volume rv -policy v_dst_pol
c12::> vol modify -vserver v_dst -volume dst_dp -policy v_dst_pol
c12::> vol mount -vserver v_dst -volume dst_dp -junction-path /dst_dp

c11::> nfs on -vserver v_src
c11::> vserver nfs modify -vserver v_src -showmount enabled
c12::> nfs on -vserver v_dst
c12::> vserver nfs modify -vserver v_dst -showmount enabled

5. On Linux, create mountpoints and view the exported volumes.

root:/ # mkdir /mnt/210 ; mkdir /mnt/212
root:/ # showmount -e 192.168.4.210
Export list for 192.168.4.210:
/        (everyone)
/src_dp (everyone)
root:/ # showmount -e 192.168.4.212
Export list for 192.168.4.212:
/dst_dp (everyone)
/        (everyone)

6. Mount the volumes and put some files in the source volume.

root:/ #  mount 192.168.4.210:/ /mnt/210
root:/ #  mount 192.168.4.212:/ /mnt/212
root:/ # cd /mnt/210/src_dp
root:/mnt/210/src_dp # touch a b c d
root:/mnt/210/src_dp # cd /

7. Run a snapmirror update.

c12::> snapmirror update -destination-path v_dst:dst_dp
```

Now we will break the relationship, rendering the destination volume writable and we resync the relationship to maintain the DR functionality.

9.3.3 Snapmirror break and reverse sync.

---

1. Break the relationship.

```
cl2::> snapmirror break -destination-path v_dst:dst_dp
```

2. The destination volume should be writable.

```
root:/mnt/212/dst_dp # touch e
root:/mnt/212/dst_dp # ls
a   b   c   d   e
```

3. Reverse the relationship and check that the volume on cluster1 is now read-only.

```
cl1::> snapmirror create -source-path v_dst:dst_dp -destination-path
v_src:src_dp
cl1::> snapmirror resync -destination-path v_src:src_dp


root:/mnt/212/dst_dp #  cd /mnt/210/src_dp
root:/mnt/210/src_dp # touch f
touch: cannot touch 'f': Read-only file system
root:/mnt/210/src_dp # ls
a   b   c   d   e
```

To bring things back to the original state, we break again and resync. Finally we will remove the temporary relationship we created.

9.3.4 Snapmirror resync to original destination.

---

1. Break the new relationship, delete it and reestablish the original snapmirror.

```
cl1::> snapmirror break -destination-path v_src:src_d
cl1::> snapmirror delete -destination-path v_src:src_dp

cl2::> snapmirror resync -destination-path v_dst:dst_dp
```

9.4 SnapVault.

To create disk to disk backups with snapmirror, we use the XDP type. It resembles the DP variant to a great extent but has some important differences. The key-words for snapmirror XDP are *Retention* and *Snapmirror-label*. In a snapmirror XDP relationship, you can run multiple backups at different times. This means that the destination has to be able to pick one of multiple snapshots for a particular schedule. This is realized by using so-called snapmirror-labels. The source volume get a snapshot-policy in which snapmirror-labels are defined. The snapmirror relationship also gets a policy in which rules are created with a snapmirror label that matches the label in the snapshot policy of the source volume. The snapshot policy as well as the snapmirror policy can have multiple rules, so you can keep different retentions for different snapshot labels. For example, you can create hourly backups, daily backups and weekly backups, and specify different retentions.

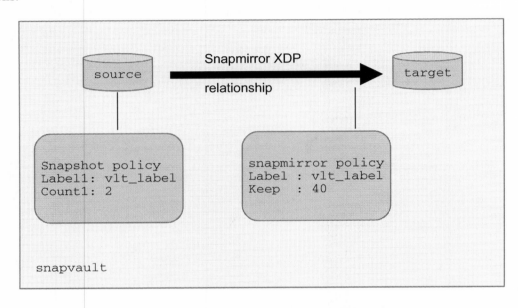

As with the DP example, we will perform a complete runthrough, including the creation and peering of the SVMs.

If you want to create an unscheduled backup, you will manually have to create a snapshot on the source volume that has a snapmirror label that matches a label in the snapmirror policy. Then you run a snapmirror update and the changes in the volume since the last scheduled backup, will be replicated. This behavior is different from a snapmirror DP relationship in that with the latter, a snapshot will automatically be created when you run a snapmirror update.

9.4.1 Snapmirror XDP setup.

```
1. Are the two clusters peered?

cl1::> cluster peer show
cl2     1-80-000008     Available   ok
cl2::> cluster peer show
cl1     1-80-000008     Available   ok

2. Create two SVMs, one on every cluster.

cl1::> vserver create v_src -subtype default -rootvolume rv -aggregate
n1_aggr1 -rootvolume-security-style unix
cl2::>  vserver create -vserver v_dst -subtype default -rootvolume rv
-aggregate aggr1 -rootvolume-security-style unix

3. Peer the two SVMs.

cl1::> vserver peer create -vserver v_src -peer-vserver v_dst -applications
snapmirror -peer-cluster cl2
cl2::> vserver peer accept -vserver v_dst -peer-vserver v_src

4. Create a source and a destination volume. The destination volume should
be of the type DP!

cl1::> vol create -vserver v_src -volume src_xdp -aggregate n1_aggr1 -size
500m -junction-path /src_xdp
cl2::> vol create -vserver v_dst -volume dst_xdp -aggregate aggr1 -size
500m -type dp

5. Create the snapmirror relationship for XDP and initialize it.

cl2::>  snapmirror create -source-path v_src:src_xdp -destination-path
v_dst:dst_xdp -type xdp
cl2::>  snapmirror initialize -destination-path v_dst:dst_xdp
cl2::>  snapmirror policy create -vserver v_dst -policy xdp_pol -type vault
cl2::>  snapmirror policy add-rule -vserver v_dst -policy xdp_pol
-snapmirror-label xdp_label -keep 5
cl2::> snapmirror modify -destination-path v_dst:dst_xdp -schedule 5min
-policy xdp_pol
```

Now the relationship has been setup, we will setup access for the Linux client, create some files and back them up.

9.4.2 Snapmirror restore.

```
1. Create the necessary Lif to access the NFS SVM and create the export-
policies.

cl1::> net int create -vserver v_src -lif nas_210 -role data -data-protocol
nfs -home-node cl1-01 -home-port e0d -address 192.168.4.210 -netmask
255.255.255.0

cl1::> export-policy create -vserver v_src -policyname v_src_pol
cl1::> export-policy rule create -vserver v_src -policyname v_src_pol
-clientmatch 0.0.0.0/0 -rorule any -rwrule any -superuser any

cl1::> vol modify -vserver v_src -volume rv -policy v_src_pol
cl1::> vol modify -vserver v_src -volume src_xdp -policy v_src_pol

2. Enable nfs.

cl1::> nfs on -vserver v_src
cl1::> vserver nfs modify -vserver v_src -showmount enabled

3. Access the volume from Linux and create some files.

root:/ # mkdir /mnt/210
root:/ # showmount -e 192.168.4.210
Export list for 192.168.4.210:
/          (everyone)
/src_xdp (everyone)
root:/ # mount 192.168.4.210:/ /mnt/210
root:/ # cd /mnt/210/src_xdp
root:/mnt/210/src_xdp #  touch a b c d

4. To run an update we create a new snapshot with the correct label.

cl1::> snap create -vserver v_src -volume src_xdp -snapshot snap1
-snapmirror-label xdp_label

cl2::> snapmirror update -destination-path v_dst:dst_xdp

5. We remove all files from the volume and restore a single file, then we
restore the whole volume.

root:/mnt/210/src_xdp # rm *

cl1::> snapmirror restore -destination-path v_src:src_xdp -source-path
v_dst:dst_xdp snap1 -file-list /a

cl1::> snapmirror restore -destination-path v_src:src_xdp -source-path
v_dst:dst_xdp snap1
```

9.5 Mirror-vault.

An *async-mirror* snapmirror policy, allows to break the relationship, thus changing the destination volume from read-only to writable. A *vault* snapmirror policy does not allow you to break the relationship. The *mirror-vault* type is a combination of DP and XDP. So you can build up retention snapshots on the destination for restoring backups, and you can break the relation for Disaster Recovery purposes.

9.6 SVMDR.

With regular snapmirror relationships, you create relationships between two volumes for DR or backup purposes. With SVMDR, you can replicate all volumes from one SVM to another SVM for disaster recovery, without managing separate volume-level relationships. By default, all volumes that you create in the source SVM, are mirrored to the destination SVM. To exclude volumes from being snapmirrored you use the **vserver-dr-protection {protected|unprotected}** argument at volume creation time.

Next to mirroring volumes, you can also mirror configuration information like, policies and network information, with the **-identity-preserve {true|false}** argument. At the snapmirror policy level, you can use the **-discard-configs network** argument. One thing that cannot be preserved is SAN configuration. The destination SVM should be configured as a *dp-destination* SVM. The destination SVM will be stopped and does not allow volume creation. Also, individual volumes cannot be snapmirrored with a snapmirror relation at the volume level.

Volumes created in the source SVM will automatically be replicated at the next update. Volumes that are removed from the source SVM will automatically be removed from the destination at the next update. Volumes that are changed into 'unprotected' will not be replicated to the destination anymore, but they will not be removed from the destination, until the source volume is removed from the source SVM.

In the next example we create two SVMs and setup a snapmirror relationship. Two volumes will be replicated, and a third volume will be excluded from replication.

9.6.1 SVMDR setup.

```
1. Are the two clusters peered?

cl1::> cluster peer show
cl2     1-80-000008    Available   ok
cl2::> cluster peer show
cl1     1-80-000008    Available   ok

2. Create two SVMs, one on every cluster. The first is of the type default,
the second is of the type dp-destination.

cl1::> vserver create v_src_dr -subtype default -rootvolume rv -aggregate
n1_aggr1 -rootvolume-security-style unix

cl2::> vserver create -vserver v_dst_dr -subtype dp-destination

3. Peer the two SVMs.

cl1::> vserver peer create -vserver v_src_dr -peer-vserver v_dst_dr
-applications snapmirror -peer-cluster cl2

cl2::> vserver peer accept -vserver v_dst_dr -peer-vserver v_src_dr

4. check the peering.

cl1::> vserver peer show
v_src_dr v_dst_dr    peered   cl2    snapmirror   v_dst_dr

5. Setup the relationship.

cl2::> snapmirror create -source-path v_src_dr: -destination-path v_dst_dr:
-type DP -identity-preserve true -schedule 5min
cl2::> snapmirror initialize -destination-path v_dst_dr:

6. Create a snapmirror policy and discard network.

cl2::> snapmirror policy create -vserver v_dst_dr -policy svmdr_pol -type
async_mirror -discard-configs network
cl2::> snapmirror modify -destination-path v_dst_dr: -policy svmdr_pol
```

The relationship has been initialized. Now the three volumes will be created.

9.6.2 SVMDR volume creation.

```
1. Create two protected volumes.

cl1::> vol create -vserver v_src_dr -volume vol1 -aggregate n1_aggr1 -size
500m -junction-path /vol1

cl1::> vol create -vserver v_src_dr -volume vol2 -aggregate n1_aggr1 -size
500m -junction-path /vol2

2. Create one unprotected volume.

cl1::> vol create -vserver v_src_dr -volume vol3 -aggregate n1_aggr1 -size
500m -junction-path /vol3 -vserver-dr-protection unprotected

3. Run a snapmirror update.

cl2::> snapmirror update -destination-path v_dst_dr:

4. Check the volumes in the destination SVM, and see that vol3 is not
there.

cl2::> vol show -vserver v_dst_dr
Vserver   Volume   Aggregate   State       Type Size  Available Used%
-------   -------  ---------   ---------   ---- ----- ---------- -----
v_dst_dr  rv       aggr2       online      RW    20MB 18.78MB     6%
v_dst_dr  vol1     aggr2       online      DP   500MB 474.8MB     5%
v_dst_dr  vol2     aggr2       online      DP   500MB 474.8MB     5%
```

Adding a volume to the source SVM will result in a new volume in the destination SVM after a snapmirror update. Removal of a volume in the source SVM will result in the removal of a volume in the destination SVM. You cannot create single volumes in the destination SVM, because it is the endpoint of a SVMDR relationship.

9.6.3 Volume protection

By default, all volumes present belonging to the source SVM will be snapmirrored to the destination SVM. Volumes that are removed from the source SVM will also be removed from the destination SVM at the next update.

You can create volumes in the source SVM that are unprotected and you an modify existing volumes in the source SVM to be unprotected. Protected volumes that are modified to *unprotected* will not be removed from the destination SVM, but snapmirror updates will not replicate the unprotected volumes anymore.

Unprotected volumes that are deleted from the source SVM, will also be deleted from the destination SVM during a snapmirror update, as are protected volumes that are removed.

9.6.4 SVMDR failover test.

To perform a DR test, we need an ip two ip-addresses and some data in the volumes. The ip's are duplicate addresses, but the destination SVM is down, so the operational state of that LIF will be down.

```
1. Create an ip-address for the SVMs.

c11::> net int create -vserver v_src_dr -lif lif1 -role data -data-protocol
nfs -home-node c11-01 -home-port e0d -address 192.168.4.226 -netmask
255.255.255.0

c12::> net int create -vserver v_dst_dr -lif lif1 -role data -data-protocol
nfs -home-node c12-01 -home-port e0c -address 192.168.4.226 -netmask
255.255.255.0 -status-admin up

2. Check the status of the Logical Interfaces, one will be up, the other
will be down.

c11::*> net int show -vserver v_src_dr -fields status-oper
v_src_dr lif1 up

c12::> net int show -vserver v_dst_dr
v_dst_dr lif1 down
```

To test the availability of the SVM on the destination cluster, we break the relationship and check the status. The sharing and accessing of volumes was discussed in paragraph 9.3.

In the following example, we will break the relationship between the to SVMs, stop the source SVM and start the destination SVM, to open up IP access and Volume access.

```
1. Break the snapmirror relationship.

c12::> snapmirror break -destination-path v_dst_dr:

2. Stop the source SVM.

c11::*> vserver stop -vserver v_src_dr

3. Start the destination SVM.

c12::> vserver start -vserver v_dst_dr
```

9.7 Synchronous Snapmirror.

In the previous paragraphs, all the relationships were of the type a-synchronous. Since ONTAP 9.5 you can also use Synchronous Snapmirror. With Synchonous Snapmirror, the client will be acknowledged that the data is safe when the data is on the destination as well as on the source. This means that there will be zero dataloss. Two types of Synchronous Snapmirror are supported: Snapmirror Sync and Snapmirror StrictSync.

With Snapmirror Sync, when the destination becomes inaccessible, the client will still be able to write to the source-volume. When the destination volumes becomes accessible again, the changed blocks will be replicated to update the destination.

With Snapmirror StrictSync, when the destination becomes inaccessible, the client will not be able to write to the source volume, until the destination becomes accessible again.

```
1. Setup a Sync relationship.

cl2::> snapmirror create -source-path v_src:src_dp -destination-path
v_dst:dst_dp -policy Sync


2. Setup a StrictSync relationship.

cl2::> snapmirror create -source-path v_src:src_dp -destination-path
v_dst:dst_dp -policy StrictSync

3. Initialize the relationship.

cl2::> snapmirror initialize -destination-path v_dst:dst_dp
```

Module 9 TRY THIS.

1. *Setup two intercluster lifs on the first cluster (cl1) and one on cluster two (cl2).*

2. *Peer the two clusters*

3 *Create two SVMs, one on each cluster.*

4. *Peer the two SVMs.*

5. *Create a source volume in the first SVM and a destination volume in the second SVM*

6. *Create a snapmirror relationship of the type DP between the two volumes and initialize the relationship.*

7. *Create a snapmirror policy and connect it to the relationship.*

8. *Break the relationship.*

9. *Remove the relationship.*

10. Flexgroups.

10.1 What is a flexgroup.

A Flexgroup is a scale-out NAS container. In fact, it is a volume that is made up of a number of constituents in multiple aggregates in the cluster so as to automatically spread the load. The FlexGroup is created with volume space-guarantee, by default. The maximum size for a FlexGroup volume in ONTAP 9.1 is 20 PB, with 400 billion files on a 10-node cluster.

There are some limitations for Flexgroups. We choose not mention them in this book because the list of limitations is bound to become smaller per ONTAP release. You can find the list on *docs.netapp.com*.

10.2 Create a flexgroup.

There are two ways to create a flexgroup. You can use the **flexgroup deploy** command. This command takes the name and the size argument and whether you want to thin provision or not. The rest is figured out by the flexgroup command itself. By default 8 constituents are created per node in the cluster, split between the two largest aggregates of every node. With All Flash Arrays one aggregate per node is used.

```
1. Create an SVM.
c12::*> vserver create v_fg -subtype default -rootvolume rv -aggregate
aggr1 -rootvolume-security-style unix

2. Deploy a flexgroup.
c12::*> flexgroup deploy -vserver v_fg -size 10g -type RW -space-guarantee
none
   (volume flexgroup deploy)

Warning: FlexGroup deploy will perform the following tasks:

        The FlexGroup will be created with the following number of
constituents of size 1.25GB: 8. The constituents will be
        created on the following aggregates: aggr2, aggr3
Do you want to continue? {y|n}: y

c12::*> vol show
Vserver     Volume      Aggregate State      Type       Size  Available Used%
---------   ---------   --------- ------     ----  ----------  ---------- -----
c12-01      vol0        aggr0     online     RW         4.16GB     3.17GB   23%
v_fg        fg          -         online     RW           10GB     9.28GB    7%
v_fg        fg__0001    aggr2     online     RW         1.25GB     1.16GB    7%
v_fg        fg__0002    aggr2     online     RW         1.25GB     1.16GB    7%
v_fg        fg__0003    aggr2     online     RW         1.25GB     1.16GB    7%
v_fg        fg__0004    aggr2     online     RW         1.25GB     1.16GB    7%
v_fg        fg__0005    aggr3     online     RW         1.25GB     1.16GB    7%
v_fg        fg__0006    aggr3     online     RW         1.25GB     1.16GB    7%
v_fg        fg__0007    aggr3     online     RW         1.25GB     1.16GB    7%
v_fg        fg__0008    aggr3     online     RW         1.25GB     1.16GB    7%
v_fg        rv          aggr1     online     RW           20MB    18.82MB    5%
11 entries were displayed.
```

You can also use the **vol create** command. This allows you to select the aggregates you want to use plus the number of constituents per aggregate. If you do not specify the size of the volume, every constituent will be 200MB.

To create 12 constituents per aggregate in a single node cluster, using three aggregates.

```
cl2::*> vol create -vserver v_fg -volume newfg -aggr-list \
aggr1,aggr2,aggr3 -aggr-list-multiplier 12

Warning: A FlexGroup "newfg" will be created with the following number of
constituents of size 200MB: 36.
Do you want to continue? {y|n}:
```

To create a 10GB flexgroup with 4 constituents per aggregate, using one aggregate per node in a single HA-Pair cluster.

```
cl1::> vol create -vserver v_fg -volume fg_vol -aggr-list n1_aggr1,n2_aggr1
-aggr-list-multiplier 8 -size 10g

Warning: A FlexGroup "fg_vol" will be created with the following number of
constituents of size 640MB: 16.
Do you want to continue? {y|n}: y
```

10.3 Resizing a flexgroup volume.

Resizing a flexgroup volume will resize all constituents equally. Obviously, if there is not enough space available in the Aggregates, the resizing will fail.

10.4 Files in constituents.

A file is not striped across constituents but is always contained in one constituent. If the file is too large for the constituent's available space, the file creation will fail. Autosizing is not supported on flexgroup volumes.

10.5 Expanding a flexgroup volume.

To add more constituents to a flexgroup volume, you can expand the volume.

```
cl1::*> vol expand -vserver v_fg -volume small_fg -aggr-list n2_aggr3
-aggr-list-multiplier 6

Warning: The following number of constituents of size 62.50MB will be added
to FlexGroup "small_fg": 6. Expanding the FlexGroup
        will cause the state of all Snapshot copies to be set to
"partial". Partial Snapshot copies cannot be restored.
Do you want to continue? {y|n}:
```

Module 10 TRY THIS.

1. Create a flexgroup volume in an available SVM, with 4 constituents in an aggregate of the first node in the cluster cl1 and 4 constituents in an aggregate of the second node. The volume size should be 4g.

2. Resize the volume to 5g. What happens to the constituents?

3. Can you set the max-autosize value for the flexgroup?

4. Can you offline individual constituents?

5. Can you move the flexgroup volume to a different aggregate?

6. Can you move an individual constituent to a different aggregate?

11. Account Management.

This module focuses on management of the cluster environment by accounts accessing the cluster or SVM for administration purposes.

11.1 Listing accounts.

```
cl1::*> security login show

Vserver: cifs_vserver
                            Authentication                Acct    Is-Nsswitch
User/Group Name   Application Method     Role Name        Locked  Group
---------------   ---------- ---------  ---------------   ------  -----------
vsadmin           http       password   vsadmin           yes     no
vsadmin           ontapi     password   vsadmin           yes     no
vsadmin           ssh        password   vsadmin           yes     no

Vserver: cl1
                            Authentication                Acct    Is-Nsswitch
User/Group Name   Application Method     Role Name        Locked  Group
---------------   ---------- ---------  ---------------   ------  -----------
admin             console    password   admin             no      no
admin             http       password   admin             no      no
(output skipped)
```

As shown in the above example, an account needs an *application*, an *authentication method* and a *role*. An account can be *locked* and an account can be a *NIS or LDAP group* to allow users from either NIS or LDAP to access the cluster or SVM. Keep in mind that an account can have multiple applications so the account may have to be created multiple times.

User accounts are connected to roles, and roles have capabilities in the form of commands with an access level.

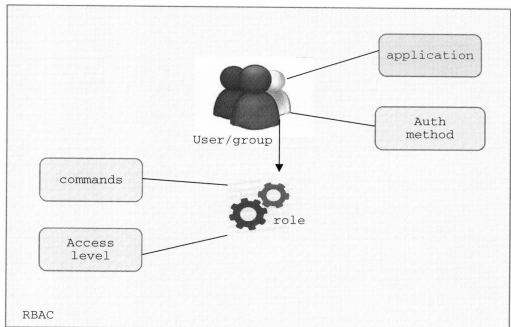

11.2 Roles.

A role can give an account access to a set of commands. There are predefined roles and roles can be created for specific purposes. A role has the following format:

cmddirname	the command or command directory to which the role has access.
access	none, readonly, and all.
query	The object that the role can access. object=*field* This is an optional argument.

11.2.1 Predefined roles.

There are some predefined roles, for the admin SVM and for the data SVMs. These roles can be modified but they cannot be deleted.

Admin SVM	Data SVM
admin	vsadmin
autosupport	vsadmin-volume
readonly	vsadmin-protocol
backup	vsadmin-readonly
none	vsadmin-snaplock
	vsadmin-backup

11.2.2 Predefined accounts.

Next to predefined roles, there are predefined accounts. These accounts can be modified but they cannot be deleted.

Admin SVM	Data SVM
admin	vsadmin
autosupport	

11.2.3 Creating accounts and roles.

As mentioned, an account needs an *application*, an *authentication method* and a *role*. This means that for every application and every authentication method and every role that you want this account to be valid for, you will have to create a separate account entry.

The following example creates an account for the *admin role* with ssh access as well as system manager access. Also, the authentication method for ssh login is *publickey* and for systemmanager login is *password*.

To access via System Manager, you will need the applications http and ontapi.

```
1. Ssh access via publickey.
cl1::> security login create -user-or-group-name view_account -application
ssh -authentication-method publickey -role admin

2. System manager access via password.
cl1::> security login create -user-or-group-name view_account -application
http -authentication-method password -role admin

cl1::> security login create -user-or-group-name view_account -application
ontapi -authentication-method password -role admin
```

Imagine you need a user to be able to manage qtrees, you will need a role that allows the creation and removal of qtrees. The user will need to be able to select a volume, so he or she will have should be allowed to read volume information. In order to facilitate that you create a role first and then a user that is able to login with ssh and with systemmanager and connect the user to the role. The SVM needs a LIF with the management firewall policy.

```
We will use an existing SVM: v_iscsi and an existing LIF iscsi_211, with address 192.168.4.211.
1. Create the roles.

cl1::*> role create -role qtree -cmddirname "volume qtree" -access all
-vserver v_iscsi

cl1::*> role create -role qtree -cmddirname "volume " -access readonly
-vserver v_iscsi

2. create the account for ssh.

cl1::> security login create -user-or-group-name q_user -application ssh
-authentication-method password -role qtree -vserver v_iscsi

3. Prepare the LIF for management access.

cl1::> net int modify -vserver v_iscsi -lif iscsi_211 -firewall-policy mgmt
```

11.3 Domain authentication.

To allow Active Directory domain accounts to manage ONTAP, whilst logging in with their actual AD password, you can setup a *domain tunnel* and accounts with *domain* authentication method in place.

1. Create an SVM.
```
cl1::*> vserver create -vserver v_tunnel -rootvolume rv -rootvolume-
security-style unix -aggregate n1_aggr1
```

2. Create an LIF in the SVM.
```
cl1::*> net int create -vserver v_tunnel -lif tunnel_224 -role data -data-
protocol cifs -home-node cl1-01 -home-port e0d -address 192.168.4.224
-netmask 255.255.255.0
```

3. Create a dns entry for the SVM.
```
cl1::*> dns create -vserver v_tunnel -domains netapp.local -name-servers
192.168.4.247
```

4. Create cifs.
```
cl1::*> vserver cifs create -vserver v_tunnel -cifs-server TUNNEL -domain
netapp.local
```

5. Create the tunnel.
```
cl1::*> security login domain-tunnel create -vserver v_tunnel
```

6. Create the domain account.
```
cl1::*> security login create -user-or-group-name netapp\administrator
-application ssh -authentication-method domain -role admin
```

7. Login from your windows cmd tool.
```
c:\> plink netapp\administrator@192.168.4.200
password:******
```

11.4 Public-key access.

When logging into the cluster, you use a valid accountname and a password. It is possible to log in without having to specify a password. This is especially desirable when you want to use scripts to execute consecutive commands without having to enter the password before each command.

You can create a public-key entry and define public-key as the authentication method for the account in question.

In the following example we create an account called *monitor* that logs in using the public-key.

```
Logged in as user pi in Linux.
pi@pi158:~$ whoami
pi


1. Check for the existence of a public-key.
pi@pi158:~$ ls .ssh/*pub
.ssh/id_rsa.pub


2. If the key does not exist, run ssh-keygen to create one.
pi@pi158:~$ ssh-keygen -t rsa
Generating public/private rsa key pair.
Enter file in which to save the key (/home/pi/.ssh/id_rsa):
Enter passphrase (empty for no passphrase): <enter>
Enter same passphrase again: <enter>
Your identification has been saved in /home/pi/.ssh/id_rsa.


3. Load the key in a buffer.
pi@pi158:~$ cat .ssh/id_rsa.pub
ssh-rsa
AAAAB3NzaC1yc2EAAAADAQABAAABAQDVPDWSPucQodAowVbY0qLdrXAoAW0yC9M9m9sSSVpU
bhzQGdST6AtbzSvRNU3MVGHSu+e0nYn70W4cG+2BFXNSUSuG1JfLYuscvwef+uLgZSDpZv37HUi
AASXoowQl1BjXsiM7+FXg/sw0R+U6mr8opkyJme289X6wHYtPme7YQqFtq7WDaNUjpxKu7FfO51
+Lv5yX2PciSxPkjHge2eOUORiuMOKxQCGRFJ+gRY7RqdU8TDjQQgzlhkjnnSrceRxaV2JBgL5j/
8XfVJzv5jx3o5rVfwY4H6ml8TxQEtocEiOQkqzbfqMQMVtAT5pyYNGsvz5uhZB18GjpT2mmZDY5
pi@pi158


Note: select the key from ssh-rsa upto and including pi@pi158 an buffer it.


Create an account in ONTAP.
cl1::*> security login create pi-account -application ssh -authentication-
method publickey -role admin

4. Create the key in ONTAP.
cl1::*> security login publickey create -username pi-account -index 0
-publickey "ssh-rsa
AAAAB3NzaC1yc2EAAAADAQABAAABAQDVPDWSPucQodAowVbY0qLdrXAoAW0yC9M9m9sSSVp
UbhzQGdST6AtbzSvRNU3MVGHSu+e0nYn70W4cG+2BFXNSUSuG1JfLYuscvwef+uLgZSDpZv37HU
iAASXoowQl1BjXsiM7+FXg/sw0R+U6mr8opkyJme289X6wHYtPme7YQqFtq7WDaNUjpxKu7FfO5
1+Lv5yX2PciSxPkjHge2eOUORiuMOKxQCGRFJ+gRY7RqdU8TDjQQgzlhkjnnSrceRxaV2JBgL5j
/8XfVJzv5jx3o5rVfwY4H6ml8TxQEtocEiOQkqzbfqMQMVtAT5pyYNGsvz5uhZB18GjpT2mmZDY
5 pi@pi158"


5. Login from Linux.
pi@pi158:~$ ssh pi-account@cl1
cl1::>
```

Module 11 TRY THIS.

1. Login as admin to the cluster 'cl1'
Create a role 'volread' that gives access to the volume command with
readonly access. The role is created in the testvserver.

2. Create a user in the testvserver that is connected to the role 'volread'
and has authmethod 'passwd'.

3. Create a lif 'm_lif' with the firewall-policy 'mgmt' and address
192.168.4.213 for SVM testvserver.

4. From Linux, login to the testvserver as 'voluser' and try the following
commands:

>   *1 vol show*
>   *2 vol offline*
>   *3 vol create*
>   *4 vol qtree show*

Which commands do not give an error?

5. Logout from the cluster and login again as admin.
Remove the role 'volread' from the SVM 'testvserver' and logout again.

6. Login as voluser to the testvserver.
Does the command 'vol show' still work?

12. Monitoring and Troubleshooting.

There are quite a few tools to monitor the ONTAP environment. Some of these tools are provided by Netapp, like *On Command Unified Manager* and *Insight Balance*. Some of these tools are opensource like *Grafana*. Next to that NetApp offers a software development kit (SDK), which you can download from *https://mysupport.netapp.com*. The *NetApp Manageability SDK* provides resources to develop applications that monitor and manage NetApp storage systems. *SDK Help* provides information about core APIs, which provide infrastructure to invoke ONTAP APIs.

This module does not cover these additional tools, but focuses on the command-line interface, as does the rest of this book. Because of the overlap between monitoring and troubleshooting, this module intends to cover the basic overview of both.

12.1 vol0.

The root volume of each node is a vital part of every cluster. If you 'lose' that volume, the node will no longer function properly, and vol0 will have to be recreated[1].

To monitor *vol0*, you may want to check the capacity of the volume. If this volume runs out of space, all configuration attempts will fail because there is no more room to store these configuration changes.

```
From the clustershell
cl1::*> cl1::*> df -h vol0 -fields percent-used-space
vserver volume fs-type percent-used-space
------- ------ ------- ------------------
cl1-01  vol0   active  26%
cl1-01  vol0   snapshot 0%
cl1-02  vol0   active  26%
cl1-02  vol0   snapshot 0%
4 entries were displayed.

cl1::*> vol show -vserver cl1-01 -volume vol0 -fields used,available
vserver volume available used
------- ------ --------- ------
cl1-01  vol0   4.22GB    1.48GB

From the nodeshell.
cl1-01> df -h vol0
Filesystem                 total      used      avail capacity Mounted on
/vol/vol0/                 5836MB    1524MB    4312MB      26% /vol/vol0/

From the systemshell
df -h /mroot
Filesystem                          Size   Used  Avail Capacity Mounted
on
localhost:0x80000000,0xec662176     5.7G   1.5G   4.3G      25%  /mroot
```

Note: the minimum size of vol0 depends on the controller type, and the chance that it will fill up reduced to a minimum. Nonetheless it is not a bad idea to figure out what is in there and what you need to be in there. Think of snapshots, for example.

---

1 From the BootMenu the command *create_temp_root* will create a new node root volume

12.2 Regenerate vol0.

In the unlikely event that you lose vol0, it can be regenerated. In the following procedure, the disks that hold aggr0 of node2 will be removed and a new vol0 will be created.

This example will need some Systemshell access. And also, this example requires root access in the systemshell. To get root access in the systemshell:

```
cl1::> set d
cl1::*> systemshell -node cl1-02
  (system node systemshell)
diag@169.254.106.90's password:

Warning:  The system shell provides access to low-level
diagnostic tools that can cause irreparable damage to
the system if not used properly.  Use this environment
only when directed to do so by support personnel.

cl1-02% sudo bash
bash-3.2# id
uid=0(root) gid=0(wheel) groups=0(wheel),5(operator)
```

Make sure you follow the above procedure when in the Systemshell.

12.2.1 debug vreport.

As discussed before, the replicated databases are in sync in the cluster. They reflect the actual configuration on every node in the cluster. But the actual LIFS and Volumes are local to each node of course. Discrepancies may occur between the RDBs and the actual situation on the node. For example: the VLDB may hold information on an aggregate or a volume that is not really there anymore in WAFL. The other way around is also possible: a volume is created in WAFL but not from the clustershell, so VLDB is not updated.

With the command **debug vreport show** you can list the inconsistencies. Ideally, there is consistency. The command is run in diag mode:

```
cl1::*> debug vreport show
This table is currently empty.

Info: WAFL and VLDB volume/aggregate records are consistent.
```

But if vol0-problems hit the fan, you will have to repair.

12.2.2 Regenerate vol0 example.

Vol0 can be regenerated when lost. What you lose when you lose vol0 is the logfiles that were local to that node. The RDB's will be retrieved from the surviving nodes in the cluster. Regenerating vol0 means that you will have to use a Spare disk to form a new temporary root, which you can later rename, after you have removed the original root aggregate.

Note: It needs be stated here, that in a simulated environment you have to make a translation to the disk devices known in ONTAP and the devices at the simulator level. The match between the two devices is made by matching the serialnumber. This is not necessary in a real live situation.

An example in 10 steps.

1. list the disks that are part of aggr0 on node2
2. get the serialnumber of every disk in aggr0
3. match the serialnumber to the disk devices in the systemshell
4. locate a spare disks assigned to node2 to become the new root
5. match the serialnumber of the spare disks to the device in the systemshell
6. from the systemshell, remove the aggr0 devices
7. reboot the node
8. enter the bootmenu, create a temporary rootvolume and boot the node
9. repair the RDB (VLDB)
10. reboot and complete the new aggregate

Note: device names may differ.

```
1. List the disks of aggr0 node2
cl1::*> aggr show -aggregate aggr0_n2
Disks for First Plex: NET-1.69, NET-1.71,
                      NET-1.72, NET-1.68

2. get the serial number of each disk.
cl1::*> disk show -disk NET-1.69 -fields serial-number
NET-1.69 11203500

cl1::*> disk show -disk NET-1.68 -fields serial-number
NET-1.68 11593504

cl1::*> disk show -disk NET-1.70 -fields serial-number
NET-1.70 11593505
```

The serialnumber of the disks is needed to locate the real device. The first two characters of the serialnumber will be removed to map to the real device name in the Systemshell.

```
3. from the systemshell  match the disk with the disks in the systemshell.
bash-3.2# cd /sim/dev/,disks
bash-3.2# ls |grep -e 203500 -e 593504 -e 593505 -e 203501
v0.16:NETAPP___:VD-4000MB-FZ-520:13203500:8248448
v0.17:NETAPP___:VD-4000MB-FZ-520:13203501:8248448
v1.20:NETAPP___:VD-4000MB-FZ-520:15593504:8248448


4. from the clustershell find a spare disk for the temproot.
cl1::*> disk show -container-type spare -node cl1-02
NET-1.57              3.93GB     - 24 FCAL    spare      Pool0      cl1-02


5. from the clustershell get the serialnumber and match it to the systemshell devicename.
cl1::*> disk show -disk NET-1.57 -fields serial-number
NET-1.57 11373507

from the systemshell match the device
cl1-02% ls |grep 373507
v3.24:NETAPP___:VD-4000MB-FZ-520:10373507:8248448
```

All relevant devices are removed from UNIX (systemshell). Make sure you also remove the entries in the file that holds the diskshelf info: `Shelf:DiskShelf14`.

```
6. From the systemshell remove the four aggr0 disks from the ,disks directory and from the shelf-file.
bash-3.2# rm v1.20\:NETAPP___\:VD-4000MB-FZ-520\:15593504\:8248448
bash-3.2# rm v0.16\:NETAPP___\:VD-4000MB-FZ-520\:13203500\:8248448
bash-3.2# rm v0.17\:NETAPP___\:VD-4000MB-FZ-520\:13203501\:8248448

Note: also remove these lines from the Shelf file Shelf:DiskShelf14.

Remove the following file: /sim/dev/,disks/,reservations. This is to prevent a panic during reboot.
bash-3.2# rm /sim/dev/,disks/,reservations
```

In step 8 a new vol0 is created on disk v3.24. Since this is done from the Boot Menu, and not from the clustershell, the VLDB is not updated. The new root volume is created directly in WAFL. This results in inconsistencies between the VLDB and the actual situation on the node.

In step 9 VLDB is repaired. The actual situation is ruling. This means that if a volume is not there in WAFL, its presence will also be removed from VLDB and if a volume is present in WAFL and not in VLDB, it will be added to VLDB to reflect the actual situation.

```
7. reboot the node.
cl1::*> node reboot -node cl1-02

8. Type CTRL+C to get to the BootMenu and run the create_temp_root command.
Selection (1-8)? create_temp_root temproot v3.24

Choose Normal boot, to boot your system.

9. repair rdb
cl1::debug vreport*> show
aggregate Differences:
(output skipped)
aggr0_n2              Present both in VLDB and WAFL with differences
                          Node Name: cl1-02
                          Aggregate UUID: bf1f332b-30ab-474c-bb42-
14193365a99b

                          Aggregate State: failed
                          Aggregate Raid Status: raid_dp, partial
                          Aggregate HA Policy: cfo
                          Is Aggregate Root: true
   Differing Attribute: Volume Count (Use commands 'volume add-other-volume'
and 'volume remove-other-volume' to fix 7-Mode volumes on this aggregate)
      WAFL Value: 0
      VLDB Value: 1

temproot(06196eed-9a2b-4acd-a22b-f9a240fa66e9)
                      Present in WAFL Only
(output skipped)

cl1::debug vreport*> fix -type volume -object temproot(06196eed-9a2b-4acd-
a22b-f9a240fa66e9)
cl1::debug vreport*> volume add-other-volume -node cl1-02
cl1::*> volume remove-other-volume -vserver cl1_02
```

```
10. Reboot node2 and complete the new root aggregate.
cl1::*> aggr delete -aggregate aggr0_n2
cl1::*> aggr rename -aggregate temproot -newname aggr0_n2
cl1::*> aggr add-disks -aggregate aggr0_n2 -diskcount 2
```

12.3 Cluster health.

To monitor the health of a cluster you can run the **cluster show** command. When at the admin privilege level, it will report the health and eligibility. Eligibility *true* means that the node is eligible to take part in the cluster. If you set this value to *false*, the node is not eligible to take part in the cluster. This is typically the case if a node is out of order for a longer period of time. You can compare it to setting a node in maintenance mode.

```
cl1::> cluster show
Node                   Health  Eligibility
---------------------- ------- ------------
cl1-01                 true    true
cl1-02                 true    true
```

Running the same command when in advanced mode, the *Epsilon* column is added. In a multi HA-Pair cluster, the Epsilon in used as a tiebreaker in case of loss of heartbeat.

12.3.1 Majority vote.

The basic rule for UNIX clustering has been one of majority vote, for a long time. This means that a node will only run in the cluster if it can establish more than half of all possible votes (partners) in the cluster.

Example:
In a four-node cluster, there is a total of 4 votes. When all nodes are up and running and every node can contact all other nodes via the cluster interconnect, the vote-count will be 4, which is more than half. In the case of a cluster interconnect failure on both interfaces if one of the nodes. That node would have a vote-count of 1, the other nodes would have 3. This would result in that single node to stop servicing data, because it drops below the majority vote count.

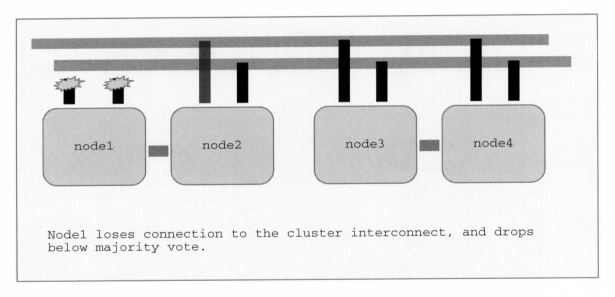

Node1 loses connection to the cluster interconnect, and drops below majority vote.

In the case of a network failure that splits the cluster in two equal partitions, both HA-Pairs would stop functioning because both would drop below majority vote:

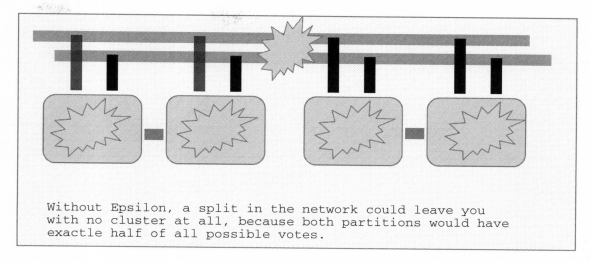

```
Without Epsilon, a split in the network could leave you
with no cluster at all, because both partitions would have
exactle half of all possible votes.
```

With the Epsilon in place, one HA-Pair would survive, and the cluster would still be up and running.

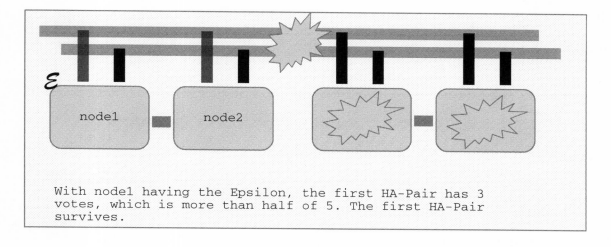

```
With node1 having the Epsilon, the first HA-Pair has 3
votes, which is more than half of 5. The first HA-Pair
survives.
```

12.3.2 Change the Epsilon node.

You can change the epsilon node manually. Obviously, you can only change the epsilon if you are 'in the cluster'.

```
cl1::*> cluster show
Node                     Health   Eligibility    Epsilon
-------------------- -------- ------------   ------------
cl1-01                   true     true           true
cl1-02                   true     true           false
cl1-03                   true     true           false
cl1-04                   true     true           false
4 entries were displayed.

cl1::*> cluster modify -node cl1-01 -epsilon false
cl1::*> cluster modify -node cl1-03 -epsilon true
```

12.3.3 Two-node cluster and Epsilon.

A single HA-Pair that forms a cluster, cannot have an Epsilon node. This would compromise the other node if the Epsilon node failed. Therefore, a single HA-Pair should use a different way to establish majority vote. In a two-node cluster, mailbox disks are used. The storage system always selects the parity disk and the first data disk of the root aggr to be the two mailbox disks in a RAID4 configuration. If the aggr is Raid-DP, then the Parity and the D-Parity disks will be selected. These mailbox disks are used to determine if a node is still up and running or not. The nodes constantly write to their own mailbox disks and check the disks of the other node. An MB disk is another way to determine the state of the partner. If the interconnect fails, the cluster can still determine if the partner is alive or not.

To disable the use of Epsilon and enable the mailbox disks you run the **ha modify -configure** command.

```
cl1::*> ha modify -configure true
   (cluster ha modify)

Warning: High Availability (HA) configuration for cluster
         services requires that both SFO storage failover and
         SFO auto-giveback be enabled. These actions will be
         performed if necessary.
Do you want to continue? {y|n}: y
```

12.3.3 Check cluster interconnect.

To check the cluster interconnect you can run the **cluster ping-cluster** command from the advanced mode. In the following example, all cluster interconnect interfaces are pinged from node1. All paths are ok.

```
cl1::*> cluster ping-cluster -node cl1-01
Host is cl1-01
Getting addresses from network interface table...
Cluster cl1-01_clus1 cl1-01    e0a       169.254.167.212
Cluster cl1-01_clus2 cl1-01    e0b       169.254.108.205
Cluster cl1-02_clus1 cl1-02    e0a       169.254.106.90
Cluster cl1-02_clus2 cl1-02    e0b       169.254.188.236
Local = 169.254.167.212 169.254.108.205
Remote = 169.254.106.90 169.254.188.236
Cluster Vserver Id = 4294967293
Ping status:
....
Basic connectivity succeeds on 4 path(s)
Basic connectivity fails on 0 path(s)
................
Detected 1500 byte MTU on 4 path(s):
    Local 169.254.108.205 to Remote 169.254.106.90
    Local 169.254.108.205 to Remote 169.254.188.236
    Local 169.254.167.212 to Remote 169.254.106.90
    Local 169.254.167.212 to Remote 169.254.188.236
Larger than PMTU communication succeeds on 4 path(s)
RPC status:
2 paths up, 0 paths down (tcp check)
```

12.3.4 Check RDBs.

One of the nodes in a cluster is the master of an RDB ring or of multiple RDB rings. One node can be the master of all five RDB rings. The master of a ring is chosen automatically by an election protocol. To monitor the health of the RDBs you run the following command in the advanced mode.

```
cl1::*> cluster ring show
Node       UnitName Epoch    DB Epoch DB Trnxs Master    Online
---------  -------- -------- -------- -------- --------- ---------
cl1-01     mgmt     1        1        15015    cl1-01    master
cl1-01     vldb     1        1        350      cl1-01    master
cl1-01     vifmgr   1        1        66559    cl1-01    master
cl1-01     bcomd    1        1        97       cl1-01    master
cl1-01     crs      1        1        41       cl1-01    master
cl1-02     mgmt     1        1        15015    cl1-01    secondary
cl1-02     vldb     1        1        350      cl1-01    secondary
cl1-02     vifmgr   1        1        66559    cl1-01    secondary
cl1-02     bcomd    1        1        97       cl1-01    secondary
cl1-02     crs      1        1        41       cl1-01    secondary
10 entries were displayed.
```

12.3.5 Recover RDBs.

In the case of one or multiple RDBs going offline, you can recover the node by restarting all the daemons on the unhealthy node, so that the RDBs of a healthy node will be synchronized with the failed node. The command should be executed from a healthy node.

In the following example, it is clear that node2 is offline where the RDBs are concerned. The recovery command will restart all relevant daemons on the node to synchronize the RDBs.

```
cl1::*> cluster ring show
Node        UnitName Epoch      DB Epoch DB Trnxs Master      Online
---------   -------- --------   -------- -------- ---------   ---------
cl1-01      mgmt     1          1        15057    cl1-01      master
cl1-01      vldb     1          1        350      cl1-01      master
cl1-01      vifmgr   1          1        66582    cl1-01      master
cl1-01      bcomd    1          1        97       cl1-01      master
cl1-01      crs      1          1        41       cl1-01      master
cl1-02      mgmt     0          1        15027    -           offline
cl1-02      vldb     1          1        350      -           offline
cl1-02      vifmgr   1          1        66582    -           offline
cl1-02      bcomd    1          1        97       -           offline
cl1-02      crs      1          1        41       -           offline
10 entries were displayed.

cl1::*> configuration recovery cluster sync -node cl1-02
   (system configuration recovery cluster sync)

Warning: This command will synchronize node "cl1-02" with the cluster configuration,
potentially overwriting critical cluster configuration files on the node. This
feature should only be used to recover from a disaster. Do not perform any other
recovery operations while this operation is in progress. This command will cause all
the cluster applications on node "cl1-02" to restart, interrupting administrative
CLI and Web interface on that node.
Do you want to continue? {y|n}: y

All cluster applications on node "cl1-02" will be restarted. Verify that the cluster
applications go online.
```

To test this procedure in the simulator, login to the systemshell and *sudo bash* to become root. Then run this command: `/etc/netapp_mroot_unmount`. This will unmount vol0 and thus make the RDBs unavailable.

12.4 Configuration backups.

By default three jobs are scheduled to create *8hourly*, *daily* and *weekly* backups. These backups are stored in **/mroot/etc/backups/config/** *(accessible from the systemshell)*. The number of backups of each backuptype is configurable.

Backup retention can be scheduled for 8hourly, daily and weekly backups. In the following example, 2 backups of every type are retained. These backups are uploaded to an ftp-server with username **mon**. User mon has a password on the ftp-server, so this should be pre-configured as well for the upload to succeed.

```
cl1::*> configuration backup settings modify -numbackups1 2 -numbackups2 2
-numbackups3 2 -destination ftp://192.168.4.240 -username mon

cl1::*> configuration backup setting set-password
   (system configuration backup settings set-password)

Enter the password: ********
Confirm the password: ********
```

Backups are stored in *7z* format. A single node cluster contains a backup of the configuration as well as of the RDBs. The **cluster_replicated_records only** contains the RDB's that can be found in the RDB directory: **/mroot/etc/cluster_config/rdb/**. The node backup contains the remaining configuration info, like parts of **/mroot/etc/** contents and **/cfcard**.

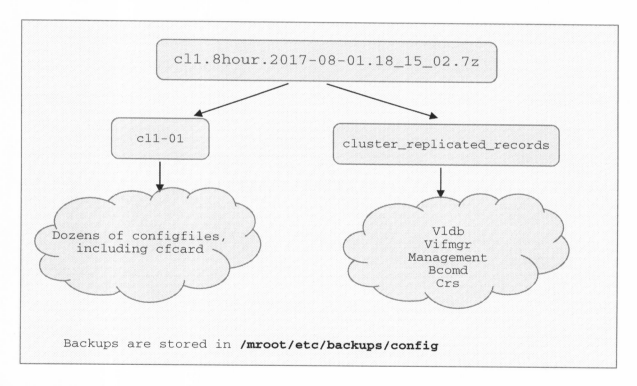

It is not very likely that you will ever have to restore a backup. As long as you have one node in the cluster up and running, and the node is healthy, you can always *resync* other nodes with the configuration from the healthy node. Only in the case of a 'total disaster' will you need to restore a backup, which will restore the node to a single node cluster.

If you want to restore a backup, you can either restore it from *vol0* or you can download it from the ftp-server, as demonstrated in the following example.

```
c11::*> configuration backup download -node c11-01 -source \
ftp://192.168.4.240/c11.8hour.2017-08-01.18_15_02.7z
   (system configuration backup download)

Enter the username: mon

Enter the password: ********
```

12.5 Autosupport.

Autosupport is an important tool for monitoring problems of any kind in your environment. Autosupport will trigger messages to Netapp and other (configurable) destinations. Also, every week, by default, NetApp will receive your cluster's configuration and health. It is best practice to enable autosupport.

To configure autosupport, this is a possible flow of actions for further setting up autosupport.

Configure dns for the admin vserver	To resolve addresses outside your network
Configure a routing entry for the admin vserver	To access addresses outside your network
Configure autosupport	To mail to the correct recipients via the correct smtp host (https and http is also supported)
Create filters	To finetune the exact messages you the right recipients.

An example:

```
1. Create or modify a dns entry for the admin vserver
cl1::*> dns create -vserver cl1 -domains mycompany.nl. -name-servers
192.168.4.1
cl1::*> dns modify -vserver cl1 -domains mycompany.nl. -name-servers
192.168.4.1

2. Create a default route for the admin vserver.
cl1::*> route create -vserver cl1 -destination 0.0.0.0/0 -gateway
192.168.4.1

3. Enable autosupport for all nodes in the cluster.
cl1::*> autosupport modify -node * -support enable -transport smtp -mail-
host smtp.mycompany.nl -from mon@mycompany.nl -to monitor@gmail.com -state
enable

4. Test autosupport.
cl1::*> cl1::> system node autosupport invoke  cl1-01 -type test

5. Create a filter and a rule.
cl1::*> event filter create -filter-name clonefilter
cl1::*> event filter rule add -filter-name clonefilter -type include
-severity INFORMATIONAL -message-name wafl.volume.clone.created
```

It is possible to create filters to further specify which messages are sent to which emails. The filter that is created in step 5, is one of more than 6000 message-names. Message-names can be included or excluded to finetune your reporting.

List all message-names:

```
cl2::> event filter rule add -filter-name fa -type include -message-name ?
   AccessCache.NearLimits
   AccessCache.ReachedLimits
   CR.Data.File.Inaccessible
   CR.Del.CrptStreamData.Fail
   CR.Del.CrptStreamRedir.Fail
   CR.Del.DangStreamData.Fail
   CR.Del.DangStreamRedir.Fail
   CR.Fix.Corrupt.Redir.Failed
   CR.Fix.Crpt.Data.Dir.Failed
  (output skipped)
```

To list all message-names:

```
cl1::> event catalog show
Message                            Severity          SNMP Trap Type
------------------------------     ----------------  ------------------
AccessCache.NearLimits             ALERT             Severity-based
AccessCache.ReachedLimits          EMERGENCY         Severity-based
CR.Data.File.Inaccessible          NOTICE            Severity-based
 (output skipped)
zsm.socket.listener.setoption      NOTICE            Severity-based
zsm.socket.output.event            INFORMATIONAL     Severity-based
6838 entries were displayed.
```

12.6 Coredumps.

In case of a Kernel panic, the system will dump its memory to disk in the form of a coredump file. This file can be uploaded to Netapp for analysis. If you want to generate a coredump manually there are two ways to do that.

```
1. trigger a dump from the Service Processor. This will also reboot the
   node.

2. reboot the node and create a dump when doing so.
```

```
1. using the SP.
cl1::*> system coredump trigger -node cl1-02

2. via a manual reboot.
cl1::*> node reboot -node cl1-02 -dump true
```

To view the coredumps you can run the **coredump show** command, or list the contents of the **/mroot/etc/crash** directory from the systemshell.

12.6.1 Upload coredumps.

Coredumps can be listed and uploaded if needed. To upload a coredump you have to specify a URL, as with uploading backups. By default coredumps are automatically uploaded to the a NetApp ftp-server. The following output lists the default ftp-server and one that was modified by the **coredump config modify** command.

```
cl1::*> coredump config show
(system node coredump config show)
                                         Autosave
        Sparse      Min      Max      Max On
        Core       Free     Dump     Save Startup
Node    Enabled    Bytes Attempts Attempts Enabled Coredump Location
-----   -------   -------- -------- -------- -------
----------------------------
cl1-01
        true       250MB        2        2 true     ftp://ftp.netapp.com/to-
ntap/
cl1-02
        true       250MB        2        2 true     ftp://192.168.4.240
```

Appendix A Answerkey to TRY THIS.

Module 2 Try This.

```
1. Connect to the administrative ip-address of cluster cl1.

What does you prompt look like?
Should be something like: cl1::>

What is the ONTAP version?
Answer: "version"

2. Press the <tab> key.

What happens?
All commands (24?) at the top level are shown.

3. Press the <?> key.

What happens?
Answer: All top-level commands are listed, but now with some explanatory
line.

4. Type "net" and press <enter>.

What happens?
Answer: The prompt changes to cl1::network>

5. Type "top" and press <enter>

What happens?
Answer: You are back at the top-level.

6. Type "set d" and press <enter>

What happens?
Answer: You enter diag-mode and your prompt will be cl1::*>

7. Type "systemshell" and press <tab>

What happens?
Answer: In a multi-node cluster you have to pick a node. Then you have to
enter the diag password.

If you did not set this password yet, what do you have to do to set is and
successfully login to the systemshell?
Answer: you have to run "security login unlock" and "security login
password".

8. Type "node run -node" and press <tab>

What happens?
Answer: you have to enter the node-name and will enter the nodeshell. Your
prompt will change from cl1::*>  to cl1-01>.
Type "exit" and press <enter> to leave the nodeshell.
```

9. Type "set admin" and press <enter>
   Type "man systemshell" and press <enter>

What happens?
Answer: you will get an error message, because the systemshell command is not available in the admin mode.

10. Type "set d" and press <enter>
    Type "man systemshell"

Now you will get the manual page.

11. Type "cluster show" and press <enter>

What happens?
Answer: you will get information on cluster health, eligibility and epsilon.

12. Type "cluster show -fields health" and press <enter>

What happens?
Answer: you will get information on the health of the clusternodes only.

Module 3 TRY THIS.

1. *Connect to the administrative ip-address of cluster cl1.*

2. *List the available space in all aggregates in the cluster.*

Answer: "aggr show -fields availsize"

3. *List all spare disks of node1.*

Answer: "disk show -container-type spare -node cl1-01"

4. *Create an aggregate "test_aggr" with a diskcount and maxraidsize of six.*

Answer: "aggr create -aggregate test_aggr -diskcount 6 -maxraidsize 6"

5. *List the parity and data disks in aggregate test_aggr.*

Answer: "disk show -aggregate test_aggr -fields position"

6. *Are any SSD's available in your configuration?*

Answer: "disk show -type SSD"

7. *list all available disktypes in your configuration.*

Answer: disk show -fields type

8. *Bring the aggregate test_aggr offline.*

Answer: "aggr offline -aggregate test_aggr"

9. *list all aggregates that are offline.*

Answer: "aggr show -state offline"

10. *Bring the aggregate test_aggr online.*

Answer: "aggr online -aggregate test_aggr"

11. Change the raidgroupsize to 8.

Answer: "aggr modify -aggregate test_aggr -maxraidsize 8"

12. Add 8 disks to aggregate test_aggr.

Answer: "aggr add -aggregate test_aggr -diskcount 8"

13. How many disks are in raidgroup rg0 and how many are in rg1?

Answer: "node run -node cl1-01 -command aggr status -r test_aggr"
        /test_aggr/plex0/rg0 has 8 disks
        /test_aggr/plex0/rg1 has 6 disks

Module 4 TRY THIS.

---

1. List all Storage Virtual Machines.

Answer: "vserver show"

2. Create a new SVM called 'testvserver' with a rootvolume called 'rv' and a rootvolume security style 'unix'.

Answer: "cl1::> vserver create -vserver testvserver -rootvolume rv -rootvolume-security-style unix -aggregate n1_aggr1"

3. Create a 100MB volume called 'datavol' in the testvserver and mount it to a junction-path with the same name.

Answer: "cl1::> vol create -vserver testvserver -volume datavol -aggregate n1_aggr1 -size 100m -junction-path /datavol"

4. Resize the new volume to 200MB.

Answer: cl1::> vol size -vserver testvserver -volume datavol -new-size 200m

5. Create a thin provisioned volume called 'thin' in testvserver of 200MB and mount it to the 'thin' junction-path.

Answer: cl1::> vol create -vserver testvserver -volume thin -aggregate n1_aggr1 -size 100m -junction-path /thin -space-guarantee none

6. Create a second SVM and move the volume datavol to the new SVM.

Answer: "vol unmount -vserver testvserver -volume datavol"
        "volume rehost -vserver testvserver -volume datavol -destination-vserver testsvm"

7. Move the volume 'datavol' to another aggregate.

Answer: "volume move start -vserver testsvm -volume datavol -destination-aggregate n2_aggr1"

8. Delete the volume 'datavol'.

Answer: "vol offline -vserver testsvm -volume datavol"
        "volume delete -vserver testsvm -volume datavol"

9. What is the delete-retention time for volumes in the SVM 'testsvm'?

Answer: "vserver show -fields volume-delete-retention-hours testsvm"

10. Remove the volume 'datavol' permanently and set the retention time to 0.

Answer: "vol recovery-queue purge -vserver testsvm -volume datavol_1057"
        "vserver modify -vserver testsvm -volume-delete-retention-hours 0"

---

11. Delete the SVM testsvm

Answer: "vol offline -vserver testsvm -volume rv"
        "vol delete -vserver testsvm -volume rv"
        "vserver delete -vserver testsvm"

Module 5 TRY THIS.

1. List all ports and their ipspace and broadcast-domain.

Answer: "net port show -fields ipspace,broadcast-domain"

2. Create a logical interface in an existing SVM and make sure the LIF only supports NFS. The ip-address is '192.168.10.10', the netmask is '255.255.255.0'. The port is e0c on node1.

Answer: "net int create -vserver testsvm -lif lif1 -role data
            -data-protocol iscsi -home-node cl1-02 -home-port e0c
            -address 192.168.10.10 -netmask 255.255.255.0"

3. List the ipspace of every SVM.

Answer: "vserver show -fields ipspace"

4. Create a route entry for the SVM 'testsvm'.

Answer: "route create -vserver testsvm -destination 0.0.0.0/0
        -gateway 192.168.4.1"

5. Create a failover-group for SVM testsvm with the e0c ports of node1 and node2.

Answer: "failover-groups create -vserver testsvm -failover-group
        testgroup -targets cl1-01:e0c,cl1-02:e0c"

6. Connect the lif you created in 2. to the failover-group 'testgroup'.

Answer: "net int modify -vserver testsvm -lif lif1
        -failover-group testgroup"

7. Migrate the lif 'lif1' to port e0c on node2.

Answer: "net int migrate -vserver testsvm -lif lif1 -destination-node cl1-02
-destination-port e0c"

8. Revert the lif back to its home-node and home-port.

Answer: "net int revert -vserver testsvm -lif lif1"

9. Change the home-node of the lif 'lif1' to node 2, and revert the lif.

Answer: "net int modify -vserver testsvm -lif lif1 -home-node cl1-02 "
        "net int revert -vserver testsvm -lif lif1"

10. Create a firewall policy that allows only ssh for all clients and
    connect the firewall policy to lif1.

Answer: "firewall policy create -vserver testvserver -policy testpol
        -service ssh -allow-list 0.0.0.0/0"
        "net int modify -vserver testvserver -lif lif1 -firewall-policy
        testpol"

Module 6 TRY THIS.

1. Create two SVMs, 'srcsvm' and dstsvm, with rootvolume 'rv', aggregate 'n1_aggr' and rootvolume security style 'unix'.

Answer: "vserver create -vserver srcsvm -subtype default -rootvolume rv
-aggregate n1_aggr1 -rootvolume-security-style unix"

2. Peer the two SVMs for the application 'snapmirror'.

Answer: "vserver peer create -vserver srcsvm -peer-vserver dstsvm
-applications snapmirror"

3. Suspend the peer relation between the two SVMs.

Answer: "vserver peer suspend -vserver dstsvm -peer-vserver srcsvm"

4. Resume the peer relation.

Answer: "vserver peer resume -vserver dstsvm -peer-vserver srcsvm"

5. Delete the two SVMs.

Answer:　"vserver peer delete -vserver srcsvm -peer-vserver dstsvm"
"volume offline -vserver srcsvm -volume rv"
"volume offline -vserver dstsvm -volume rv"
"vol delete -vserver srcsvm -volume rv"
"vol delete -vserver dstsvm -volume rv"
"vserver delete -vserver srcsvm"
"vserver delete -vserver dstsvm"

Module 7 TRY THIS.

```
1. Create a volume 'parentvol' in the SVM testvserver.

Answer: "vol create parentvol -vserver testvserver -aggregate n1_aggr1 -size
100m -junction-path  /pvol"

2. Export the volume with NFS and mount it from the linux client.

Answer: "mount 192.168.4.212:/ /mnt/212"

3. Create a file 'datafile' in the volume with content: original content.

Answer: "cd /mnt/212/pvol/"
        "echo 'original content' > pvol"

4. Create a snapshot 'parentsnap' in the volume parentvol.

Answer: "snap create -vserver testvserver -volume parentvol -snapshot
parentsnap"

5. Change the content of the file to: new content.

Answer: "echo 'new content' > datafile"


6. Restore the file from the snapshot 'parentsnap'.

Answer: snap restore-file -vserver testvserver -volume parentvol -snapshot
        parentsnap -path /datafile

7. Create a flexible clone from using the snapshot 'parentsnap' as parent
   snapshot. Make sure the clone volume is mounted on '/cvol'.

Answer: "vol clone create -vserver testvserver -flexclone clonevol -parent-
volume parentvol -parent-snapshot parentsnap -junction-path /cvol"

8. Modify the content of 'datafile' in the clone volume to 'clone content'.

Answer: "echo 'clone content' > /mnt/212/cvol/datafile"

9. Delete the snapshot 'parentsnap' from the volume 'parentvol'.
What happens?

Answer: snap delete -vserver testvserver -volume parentvol -snapshot
parentsnap
        The command will fail because the snapshot is locked.

10. Split the cloned volume.

Answer: "vol clone split start -vserver testvserver -flexclone clonevol"
```

Module 8 TRY THIS.

1. Create a volume 'nfs1' in the SVM 'testvserver' that supports the nfs
   protocol with junction-path /nfsvol

Answer: "vol create nfsvol -vserver testvserver -aggregate n1_aggr1 -size
500m -state online -junction-path /nfsvol -policy default"

2. Create an export-policy 'datapol' that allows the Linux vm to mount the
exported volume with read and write access
      and treat uid 0 as uid 0.

Answer: "export-policy create -vserver testvserver -policyname datapol"
       "export-policy rule create -vserver testvserver -policyname datapol
        -clientmatch 192.168.4.159 -rorule any -rwrule any -superuser any"
       "vol modify -vserver testvserver -volume nfsvol -policy datapol"

3. From Linux, mount the volume to the mountpoint /mnt/nfsvol
   (the testvserver has address 192.168.4.212.)

Answer: "mkdir /mnt/nfsvol ;mount 192.168.4.212:/nfsvol /mnt/nfsvol"

4. Create some files in the volume.

Answer: "touch /mnt/nfsvol/a /mnt/nfsvol/b"

5. Create a volume 'cifs1' in the SVM 'testvserver' that supports the nfs
   protocol with junction-path /cifsvol

Answer: vol create cifs1 -vserver testvserver -aggregate n1_aggr1 -size 500m
-state online -junction-path /cifsvol

6. Create a dns server and a cifs server for the SVM testvserver.
   (use your own domain-name and server IP.)

Answer: dns create -vserver testvserver -domains netapp.local -name-servers
192.168.4.247
cifs create -vserver testvserver -cifs-server CIFS1 -domain netapp.local

7. Create a cifs share for the volume 'cifs1'.

Answer: "cifs share create -share-name CIFSVOL -vserver testvserver -path
/cifsvol"

8. From the windows command-tool map a driveletter to the share.

Answer: "net use p: \\192.168.4.212\CIFSVOL

Module 9 TRY THIS.

```
1. Setup two intercluster lifs on the first cluster (cl1) and one on
   cluster two (cl2).
cl1::> net int create -vserver cl1 -lif il1 -role intercluster -home-node
cl1-01 -home-port e0c -address 192.168.4.205 -netmask 255.255.255.
cl1::> net int create -vserver cl1 -lif il2 -role intercluster -home-node
cl1-02 -home-port e0c -address 192.168.4.206 -netmask 255.255.255.0
cl2::> net int create -vserver cl2 -lif il1 -role intercluster -home-node
cl2-01 -home-port e0c -address 192.168.4.207 -netmask 255.255.255.0

2. Peer the two clusters
cl1::> cluster peer create -peer-addrs 192.168.4.207
cl2::> cluster peer create -peer-addrs 192.168.4.206

3 Create two SVMs, one on each cluster.
cl1::> vserver create -vserver v_src -subtype default -rootvolume rv
-aggregate n1_aggr1 -rootvolume-security-style unix
cl2::> vserver create v_dst -subtype default -rootvolume rv -aggregate
n2_aggr1 -rootvolume-security-style unix

4. Peer the two SVMs.
cl1::> vserver peer create -vserver v_src -peer-vserver v_dst -applications
snapmirror -peer-cluster cl2
cl2::> vserver peer accept -vserver v_dst -peer-vserver v_src

5. Create a source volume in the first SVM and a destination volume in the
second SVM
cl1::> vol create -vserver v_src -volume src -aggregate n1_aggr1 -size 100m
-state online -junction-path /src
cl2::> vol create -vserver v_dst -volume dst -aggregate n2_aggr1 -size 100m
-state online -type DP

6. Create a snapmirror relationship of the type DP between the two volumes
and initialize the relationship.
cl2::> snapmirror create -source-path v_src:src -destination-path v_dst:dst
cl2::> snapmirror initialize -destination-path v_dst:dst

7. Create a snapmirror policy and connect it to the relationship.
cl2::> snapmirror policy create -vserver v_dst -policy tstpol
cl2::> snapmirror modify -destination-path v_dst:dst -policy tstpol

8. Break the relationship.
cl2::> snapmirror break -destination-path v_dst:dst

9. Remove the relationship.
cl2::> snapmirror delete -destination-path v dst:dst
```

Module 10 TRY THIS.

1. Create a flexgroup volume in an available SVM, with 4 constituents in an aggregate of the first node in the cluster cl1 and 4 constituents in an aggregate of the second node. The volume size should be 4g.

Answer:
cl1::*> volume create -vserver testvserver -volume newfg -aggr-list n1_aggr1,n2_aggr1 -aggr-list-multiplier 4 -size 4g

2. Resize the volume to 5g. What happens to the constituents?

Answer: The constituents will grow with 250MB.

3. Can you set the max-autosize value for the flexgroup?

Answer: No.

4. Can you offline individual constituents?

Answer: Yes.

5. Can you move the flexgroup volume to a different aggregate?

Answer: No, moving flexgroups is not supported.

6. Can you move an individual constituent to a different aggregate?

Answer: Yes.
cl1::*> vol move start -vserver v_example -volume newfg__0008 -destination-aggregate test_aggr

Module 11 TRY THIS.

```
1. Login as admin to the cluster 'cl1'
Create a role 'volread' that gives access to the volume command with
readonly access. The role is created in the testvserver.

cl1::*> role create -role volread -cmddirname "volume" -access readonly
-vserver testvserver

2. Create a user in the testvserver that is connected to the role 'volread'
and has authmethod 'passwd'.

cl1::*> security login create -user-or-group-name voluser -application ssh
-authentication-method password -vserver testvserver -role volread

3. Create a lif 'm_lif' with the firewall-policy 'mgmt' and address
192.168.4.213 for SVM testvserver.

cl1::*> net int create -vserver testvserver -lif m_lif -role data -firewall-
policy mgmt -address 192.168.4.213 -netmask  255.255.255.0 -home-port e0c

4. From Linux, login to the testvserver as 'voluser' and try the following
commands:

        1 vol show
        2 vol offline
        3 vol create
        4 vol qtree show

Which commands do not give an error?

Answer: 1 and 4

5. Logout from the cluster and login again as admin.
Remove the role 'volread' from the SVM 'testvserver' and logout again.

cl1::*> role delete -role volread -cmddirname "volume" -vserver testvserver

6. Login as voluser to the testvserver.
Does the command 'vol show' still work?

Answer: testvserver::> vol show
Error: "vol" is not a recognized command
```

INDEX

Alphabetical Index

Made in United States
Orlando, FL
21 October 2023

38080051R00095